After~Dinner

Drinks

Choosing, Serving, Enjoying *After~Dinner* Drinks

JON BECKMANN

PHOTOGRAPHS BY *frankie frankeny*

CHRONICLE BOOKS
SAN FRANCISCO

Maps on pages 52 and 94 courtesy of
W. Graham Arader III Gallery, San Francisco.
Library of Congress Cataloging-in-Publication
Data available. ISBN 0-8118-2094-7
Printed in Hong Kong.

DESIGNED BY *Julia Flagg*
PHOTOGRAPHS BY *Frankie Frankeny*
FOOD STYLING BY *Wesley Martin*

The photographer wishes to thank Bill LeBlond
for once again thinking of me and Julia Flagg
for her wonderful design and collaboration with
photo and design, Wesley Martin and Alison
Richman as always, Monty Sander, Kelly Frankeny,
Cindy Blair, John Mathies, Anna Loring, Mark
Miyamoto, Erin Riley, and Sean Ellis.
In addition I would like to thank the following
in San Francisco for their time and space:
Julio Bermejo, TOMMY'S MEXICAN RESTAURANT
Ken Mc Donald, FRIENDLY SPIRITS
Ben Haller, NEIMAN MARCUS
Larry Stone, RUBICON
Traci Des Jardins, JARDINIÈRE
Loretta Keller, BIZOU
Hubert Germain-Robin, GERMAIN-ROBIN
Dirk Hampson, FAR NIENTE
Laura Bellizzi, HOTEL UTAH

Distributed in Canada by
Raincoast Books
8680 Cambie Street
Vancouver, British Columbia V6P 6M9

10 9 8 7 6 5 4 3 2 1

Chronicle Books
85 Second Street
San Francisco, California 94105

www.chroniclebooks.com

dedication

SALUT TO MY WIFE, BB;

MY MOTHER; AND RACLETTE, THE SWISS CHEESE DOG,

WHO SAT BY MY SIDE AS THESE WORDS WERE PROCESSED.

ACKNOWLEDGMENTS

I want to thank my editor Bill LeBlond for the stimulus (over a post-lunch glass of poire Williams) and his stewardship, and Sarah Putman for her intelligent and sensitive editing, and my agent, Fred Hill, for leading me to Bill and Sarah. This book is composed of too many books, articles, Web sites, and sips to acknowledge here, but I would like to point the reader who wants a more extensive listing and rating of specific brands of the postprandials described to Daniel Lerner's Single Malt & Scotch Whisky, *Gary and Mardee Haidin Regan's* The Book of Bourbon and Other Fine American Whiskeys, *and, especially, to F. Paul Pacult's excellent and exhaustive* Kindred Spirits: The Spirit Journal Guide to the World's Distilled Spirits and Fortified Wines.

TABLE OF CONTENTS

Foreword

You're approaching the end of a terrific meal— one to which, if you were a Michelin inspector, you'd give three stars. The dessert plates are cleared, the table crumbed, and the last drops of the superb Pinot Noir you selected are swallowed. Coffee is poured. The conversation is stimulating; you and your dining companions want to linger. The waiter suggests an after-dinner drink. But of course. He brings a *carte*. There are cognacs and Armagnacs and brandies. There are grappas. There are eaux de vie—pear, raspberry, cherry, plum, and two kinds of Calvados. Then there are ports, Madeiras, Sauternes, late-harvest dessert wines from America and from Europe. And single malt Scotches. Even a single-batch bourbon or two.

The mellowness, the fine feeling a good meal with good friends promotes, can be enhanced by the pleasure of an after-dinner drink. However, for the uninitiated, this moment can be the same sort of trial a formidable wine list presents to one whose familiarity with the beverage extends to the house white. After-dinner drinks are a distinct and complex element of a meal, one that has only recently engaged the interest of Americans. In Europe for hundreds of years distilled liquor has had its place at the end of the meal, not at the beginning, as is the practice in the United States.

The invention of many of these drinks has multiple roots. Historical circumstances, the search for curative elixirs, agricultural accident, politics, and religion all play a role. But probably the basic motivation was frugality: many of the libations that grace the after-dinner drink menu began as a way of using leftovers—the pomace of grapes left behind in the winemaking process, fruit that might otherwise rot. Certainly, the grape- and fruit-based spirits originated as an efficient and frugal use of the local bounty.

The waiter will not extend to our diners ordering after-dinner drinks the same ritual that is involved in ordering wine—the opportunity to taste and approve the selection—but, as with wine, the nature of each after-dinner drink is the product of many environmental factors and manufacturer's skills. The taster's eye, nose, and palate can discern the quality of the drink at hand and, just as with wine, compare it to and against other products from the same family.

A few of the factors that influence the taste of an after-dinner drink are the nature and quantity of the grain or fruit used in its production; the level of heat used for distillation (a lower heat produces a more flavorful spirit); the source of this heat (a peat fire, for example, produces the smoky flavor of Scotch); the kind of cask used for aging (oak is preferred); the duration of aging; and the effects of climate and geography, both on the ingredients and the maturation process.

So you can "taste" an after-dinner drink, just as you would do a fine wine. There will be many flavors, textures, and nuances. Evaluate its clarity and purity, aroma, flavor, and finish. Not surprisingly, the characteristics of these drinks, given their higher voltage, will be stronger and more intense than those of wine. Wine goes best with food, its subtleties enhancing the meal, and vice versa; with a few exceptions, after-dinner drinks are just that, meant to be enjoyed by themselves, postprandially.

Several classes of after-dinner drinks, particularly the eaux de vie, are thought to be aids to digestion, hence the French *digestif* and the Italian *digestivo*. The Italians, especially, have a great many *amari,* bitter, herbal, mildly alcoholic concoctions such as Fernet Branca, that would better grace a pharmacist's shelf than a dinner table. If a need for a *digestivo* arises, I would turn to Tums. Regardless of any medicinal properties the drinks in this book might possess, their reason for inclusion is the pleasure they provide.

Not everyone agrees on what is properly an after-dinner drink. I do not intend to mention in this book every drink that has served that purpose. (I have seen beer being drunk after dinner; in Italy, chilled vodka seemed popular some years ago.) And, not every contemporary after-dinner drink is reserved exclusively for a meal's finale. Scotch or bourbon often preface a meal, especially in America. Even the core after-dinner drinks have been imbibed as the sun is rising, not setting. The French workingman occasionally enjoys a shot of Calvados in his morning coffee, called a *café Calva*. Italians do the same with grappa—but it is more discreetly called a *caffé cometto*. The English of Empire days loved port at almost any time of day or night. Sherry I consider an aperitif. Champagne, the one truly all-purpose alcoholic drink, is *à propos* at breakfast, lunch, and dinner, and any time during, after, and in between.

If there is one criterion for inclusion in this book, it would be those drinks commonly found on the after-dinner drink menu in better restaurants today. The list would include fortified wines (ports and Madeiras); dessert or late-harvest wines; grape-based brandies (cognac, Armagnac, grappa, and a few American offerings); fruit-based brandies, or eaux de vie (including Calvados, the apple brandy of Normandy, which seems to occupy a niche of its own); and grain-based drinks, namely single malt Scotch and single-batch bourbon. And, last, several based on plants and herbs, which, for lack of a better term, are here called exotica.

It's a fair guess that most of us who have become acquainted with the custom of an after-dinner (or after-lunch) drink—a postprandial—did so first by having a cognac or port. Those of a certain age may remember the bygone era of sweeter, more exotic drinks than are fashionable today—Bénédictine (and its offspring B & B), Drambuie, Chartreuse, and Grand Marnier, to name a few of the better offerings. (Today, one with an inclination for the taste of Scotch after dinner would steer to a single malt rather than to Drambuie.)

I do not include liqueurs, which are to my mind best served over ice cream, and a throwback to the entertainment style of the fifties. Being of that certain age, I recall with a shiver one of the most flamboyant and bizarre of after-dinner concoctions, the infamous pousse-café. Up to fourteen liqueurs, from the heaviest or densest to the lightest in specific gravity, each a different color, were carefully poured over an inverted spoon, so they formed distinct ascending layers in the glass. The pourer might begin with crème de bananes, and move on to crème de cassis, crème de menthe, crème de cacao, apricot liqueur, blue curaçao, blackberry liqueur, peach-flavored brandy, triple Sec, rock and rye, kummel, B & B, sloe gin, and top it off with kirsch. I suspect the proper toast for such an end to the meal should not be To Your Health, but To Your Health Provider.

No one can be a devotee of every after-dinner possibility, although given enough time and the appropriate circumstances, one might sample the spectrum. I began with cognac, enjoying its silky consistency, its bouquet of grape and hints of spices, mainly vanilla, and the taste of caramel (in some cases, almost an alcoholic crème brûlée).

Then, as my taste buds (I don't question them, neither do I try to analyze them) required a drier finis to a repast, I gravitated to grappa and marc. For centuries, these high-octane distillations of fermented grape pomace kept many a peasant insulated from the winter, and in a rudimentary state could assault the nose and windpipe with the force of a snifter of Shell unleaded. But made from first-rate ingredients and prepared carefully, they are, if not as elegant as cognac (or other fine brandies), a purer presentation of the variety of grape used. Not a trace of sweetness, no flavors but the fruit. Not too long ago, grappa began to appear in the United States in exotically shaped, hand-blown bottles, and a drink that used to cost a thrifty farmer pennies now outstrips the finest cognacs in price.

In the 1970s, while traveling in France and Italy, I discovered eaux de vie, brandies made from fruit other than the grape. Calvados, the apple brandy of Normandy, I first encountered in Paris. It appears on all Paris café drink lists, and in particular I remember having, after a meal at the Brasserie Flo, an apple granita served with a shot of Calvados. It bore no resemblance to applejack—just as American fruit-based liqueurs bear no resemblance to eaux de vie. A good Calvados—some are aged for decades—is truly the elixir of apple. In Provence and Alsace, especially the latter, I found a great assortment of eaux de vie—made from raspberries, several varieties of plum, peaches, pears, cherries, and quince, to name the major flavors. In Alsace, the variety is staggering, and goes beyond fruit to the use of other vegetable and herbal materials. I think if the Alsatians had lawns they would make an eau de vie out of grass clippings. But it was in Italy that I found my favorite, poire Williams, or *eau de vie de poire.* Made in Switzerland and Italy from the Williams pear, which we call Bartlett, this essence of the fruit can be found in almost any good Continental restaurant. I had been puzzled by the presence of a whole ripe pear in many of the bottles, the mouths of which are no wider than that of a wine bottle, until a springtime visit to the area around Verona. The fruit trees had flowered, and as I drove by pear orchards, I could see empty bottles appended to the budding branches, as if the trees were producing bottles instead of fruit.

This book is neither a guide to specific brands of post-prandials, although many are mentioned, nor is it a list of ratings and rankings. It is, I hope, an enjoyable look into the origins and nature of the various drinks that make up its subject. And perhaps, when the waiter or host asks at the culmination of the meal, "Would you like an after-dinner drink?" the choice of an eau de vie or a nectar of the vine will be easy and informed.

An Ancient Art

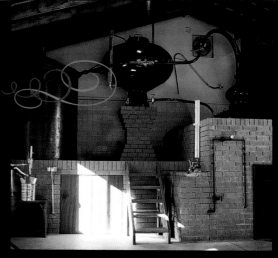

ALL THE LIQUORS—as distinct from the wines—in this book can be gathered under the inspirational phrase, "water of life" (*aqua vitae* in Latin, *eau de vie* in French; even the word "whisky" has its root in the Gaelic for "water of life"). The French refer frequently to cognac as an eau de vie (there is a University of Eaux de Vie in the town of Cognac), and all the fruit brandies are known categorically as eaux de vie. This rather lofty appellation was not inspired by the liquors' capability to warm the throats and enhance the moods of its imbibers; rather, it relates to the invention of the art of distillation and the creation of alcohol.

The word "alcohol" derives, ironically, from the Arabic, the tongue spoken by the largest group of teetotalers on earth, as does the word "alembic" or pot still, which probably originated in the Middle East during the first millennium B.C. as a result of the alchemists' desire to transform various everyday materials into something headier and nobler. This early research and development involved much heating and boiling of various liquids in the expectation of releasing medicinal elixirs. With the invention of the alembic, they found a way to capture the steamy essence of fermented liquids by subjecting them to condensation.

The water of life was created through this process of distillation. (We use the word "spirits" to refer to any form of alcoholic liquor, thus maintaining the early religious and magical connotation attached to the process of distillation.) The alchemists observed that the steam rose toward heaven as it was believed a saved soul did after shuffling off its mortal coil. The noun "spirits" is often used in conjunction with the adjective "ardent," from the Latin *ardere,* meaning to burn. No doubt the reference was to the process of heating the liquid to produce the liquor, but its colloquial use—now rare—during the past few centuries was a comment on the fiery finish, or aftertaste, of most of the available spirits.

Distillation was widely practiced in the ancient world. The Egyptians and Chaldeans probably had the technology; the Chinese made an alcoholic liquor from rice beer; and there is

evidence that arak, an anise-flavored spirit, was distilled in the East Indies 800 years before Christ. Aristotle in the fourth century B.C. observed that distillation could make seawater drinkable and that the same process could be applied to wine and other liquids.

The word "distill" comes from the Latin, *de stillare*, meaning "to drip down." This ancient and simple technology has changed little in thousands of years. Fermentation is a quite different process, by which alcohol is produced by the action of yeast on the sugars present in mash or fruit. In the distillation process, fermented mash or grape pomace or fruit juice is heated in the bottom of the still, usually made of copper. Tall stills are called patent stills, and smaller ones, such as are used to make batches of cognac, are called pot stills. Alcohol boils at 173.1 degrees Fahrenheit—a much lower boiling point than water—so it is fairly easy to produce steam, which is alcohol in the form of a gas, from the

fermented ingredients. This cloud rises to the top of the still, where it cools and condenses. Colorless and raw, the liquid that will become an eau de vie is known as the distillate or new spirit. Few would dream of drinking it at this stage. In most cases it will be distilled again and aged in wooden casks.

Spirits range widely in alcoholic potency. The proof of a drink refers to its alcohol content. A testing technique developed several centuries ago involved flambéing gunpowder with the liquor and checking the color and liveliness of the flame. A steady, blue flame indicated that a liquid contained 50 percent alcohol. This ideal ratio— neither too strong nor too weak—was set at 100. The level of proof is exactly twice that of the amount of alcohol in the drink. Your 80 proof whiskey contains 40 percent alcohol. Most distilled spirits are in the 80 to 100 proof range. Fortified wines which have had a spirit added to a still wine are mostly in 30 to 50 proof range.

part one

The Grape

After-dinner drinks made from grapes clearly pre-

dominate in popularity, variety, complexity of styles, history, and lore. They all originate with fermented wine; some are distilled, as with cognac and grappa; some are fortified with brandy, as with ports and Madeiras; and some are grown and harvested in an extraordinary way, as with sweet dessert wines—which, unless chosen as dessert itself, might more accurately be called after-dessert wines, for they only occasionally go well with a sweet course.

Geography plays a large role in the character of grape-based beverages. True cognac comes from only one small area in France; Madeira and port take their name from specific regions of Portugal; a number of sweet wines such as Sauternes, Beaumes-de-Venise, and Vin Santo are unalterably linked to place. Perhaps only single malt Scotch matches this focus on locus, an unusual distinction given its grain basis, which it shares with beer, an even more global drink than wine. When we order a glass of Chardonnay, we may get an estimable one from California, France, Italy, Australia, or even Chile, but when we order a cognac, we should get a brandy from France's Charente Valley, and no other place.

The grape is a contradictory fruit. On one hand, it is famously hardy, flourishing around the world in different climates and soils. The native American grape, *Vitis labrusca,* which is the Concord grape of jelly fame, abounded naturally without the aid of a human hand. The European wine grape, *Vitis vinifera,* while much more sensitive than its American cousin, can thrive in wet and dry, coolness and heat. It has an affinity for impoverished soils—that in which port grapes grow is literally pulverized stone and subject to climatic variations ranging from snow to midsummer temperatures well over 100 degrees Fahrenheit; champagne grapes grow out of chalk; German Riesling out of slate. There is a vine-yard saying, "The grapes like to suffer." Plentiful sun and rich soil do not make a great wine. Fine wine demands considerable attention to all the environmental factors that affect the berry to be fermented, what the French call *terroir.*

The grape has played a significant role in human history, from the cause of Noah's disgrace to its current status as a health food. Omar Khayam perhaps said it best when he included "a jug of wine" in his trinity of life's needs.

*"Claret is the liquor for boys,
port for men;*

*but he who aspires to be a hero
must drink brandy."*

—Samuel Johnson

brandy

Distilled from wine, brandy is made the world over, in places as unexpected as Bulgaria and Cyprus. Most brandies are not what the aficionado would call "serious," except for the damage they can do to one's liver.

The word "brandy" comes from the Dutch for burnt wine, *brandewijin,* an obvious reference to its mode of production. The origins of brandy no doubt are found in those of distillation. In 1250, a Frenchman, Arnaud de Villeneuve, wrote in praise of brandy's medicinal powers. The spirit's appearance as a European trade item in the late sixteenth century is thought to be the result of several factors: it survived rough sea voyages better than wine and took up less storage space. The importer could always dilute it with water at his end. When the War of the Spanish Succession prevented brandy-makers from shipping their casks of newly distilled liquor until peace was reached in 1714, they discovered that age markedly improved it, and Johnson's heroic age began.

Cognac

If brandy drinkers are heroes, cognac is reserved for the gods and goddesses. The Cognaçais observe that all cognac is brandy, but not all brandy is cognac, thus distinguishing their product from the rest of the world's—including the rest of France's. Brandy, or "burnt wine," is made in varying quality, mostly your rudimentary pain-killer. Brandy that is entitled to the name cognac comes from one French valley.

Cognac has been a drink traditionally reserved for special occasions—like champagne. Unlike champagne, it always is served after a meal and with ceremony. Cognac's appearance was accompanied by a special camaraderie and defines the end of a meal. In the old days, it was a drink to be enjoyed by men only—women were offered sherry. And to accentuate the masculine, the spirit was enjoyed in a place apart from the dining room—for the wealthy, a drawing room or library—and the final phallic fillip was a cigar to accompany the libation. Oh, and glasses. For centuries, the *ballon,* a large, short-stemmed, balloon-shaped glass, was the choice receptacle for cognac, and the liquor swirled in the warmth generated by a cradling palm. Today's experts may debate the merits and demerits of snifters, cigars, and the application of 98.6 degrees Fahrenheit, but the scene does conjure up the mystique of cognac.

The mystique extends to Cognac, the town and region. The spirit of cognac literally pervades the air and leaves a dark patina on the walls of the towns and in the cellars where the liquor is aged. Because the oak barrels in which cognac acquires its taste and color are porous, about 2 to 3 percent of the maturing cognac evaporates out into the air. This exhalation is one of the more charming aspects of the preparation of brandy. It is called "the angels' share." The angels constitute the second largest market for cognac, after the United States.

The region of Cognac is on the Atlantic coast of France in the provinces of Charente and Charente-Maritime, 200 miles southwest of Paris, fronting on the Bay of Biscay. The Gironde River forms the border between Cognac and Bordeaux to the south. The heart of cognac production is in the Charente Valley, and six *crus,* or cognac-making areas, which were delimited by the government in

1909, are arranged in roughly concentric circles from east to west. They are ranked in quality from one to six. The districts of Grande Champagne and Petite Champagne are the *premiers crus,* or best districts, because of qualities conferred by their eastern location and soil. Moving westward in diminishing rank of quality toward the bay are the *crus* or districts named Borderies, Fins Bois, Bons Bois, and Bois Communs. The names are a giveaway. As with real estate, the three things you look for in a cognac are location, location, and location. Climate, soil, water. Even the aging barrels all come from one location. Add the architect—the *maître de chai,* or master of the maturation of the raw brandy—and the result will be a fine cognac.

The region of Cognac has a long history of trade, notably for the export of salt during the Middle Ages. In 1515, a native son, François the First, became King of France. He encouraged trade by his townspeople by granting them tax breaks. The Cognaçais became primarily Protestant (Huguenot) during the Reformation. Later, the French king Henry IV protected their freedom to worship by issuing the Edict of Nantes in 1598. Almost one hundred years later, in 1685, Louis XIV, the Sun King, repealed the Edict, forcing many Huguenot Cognaçais to flee to England and Holland. Thus began an energetic trade between Cognac and its emigres for the drink that would bear the region's name. The eighteenth century, despite continual war and civil strife, saw the rise of the major cognac makers: Delamain, Hennessy, Remy Martin, and Martell. Exports to France's enemy, England, grew substantially, even if shipments had to go through third parties to avoid embargoes. In 1815, after Napoleon's exile, the market for cognac took another dramatic leap upwards, with new producers such as Hine, Monnet, Otard-Dupuy, and Courvoisier setting up shop to meet the demand. Through the 1860s business boomed; the Dutch, the Russians, and even Latin Americans were big fans of the best of the burnt wines.

Pride—or perhaps, success— goeth before a fall. In 1871, at the height of boom times in Cognac, devastation struck the vines in the form of phylloxera, a louse that attacks grapevine roots. Exports declined, fortunes were lost, and after several hundred years of booming trade, cognac-makers faced bust. Producers of cheap brandy from other countries took advantage of the situation by calling their stuff cognac (the same fate suffered a few decades ago by French

Chablis, a perfectly fine wine, when any cheap, white, and grapey American plonk got labeled Chablis). Rescue of Cognac's vines came from the United States in 1888, when a French scientist brought back from the town of Denison, Texas, a louse-resistant rootstock. (Denison is now Cognac's sister city.) Cognac rebounded, and in 1909 the French government decreed that only brandy from the Charente region could legally be called cognac.

The making of cognac begins, contrary to what one might think from observing its amber color and sampling its sharply nuanced and rich taste, with white grapes. All cognac is by definition and decree made from white grapes—in fact, from white grapes that otherwise make a thin, unsatisfactory wine. French law stipulates that wines to be distilled into cognac be made at least 90 percent from Folle Blanche, Ugni Blanc, and Colombard grapes. Folle Blanche was once the grape of choice—as it still is, for the most part, in the making of Armagnac—but has been predominantly replaced by the higher yielding, more acidic, and less potent Ugni Blanc. Following the harvest in October, three weeks are allowed for the pomace (crushed grapes, including skins and pips) to ferment into a lowly, weak (8 percent alcohol) wine. Then the process of transcendence begins.

Tankers take the wine to the distiller, where distillation is started in November. By law, this phase must be completed by April 30, to begin the aging process before the weather turns warm. The first of several key steps in the tradition of cognac-making is hand-regulated, small batch distillation, unchanged in technique since the Europeans' adoption during the Crusades of the alembic. A small, acid-resistant copper still called the Charentais pot still is heated on an open fire of wood or coal. The wine is heated, vaporized, and then condensed in a coil—or worm—surrounded by cold water.

This conversion of wine into spirit takes place in two operations, which makes the production of cognac distinct from other brandies. The first step, the *première chauffe,* is followed by the second, the *bonne chauffe.* In each case a distillate is made, but each step is separated into two parts. The *première chauffe* is composed of the "heads" and the middle distillate, the *brouillis,* which has a pronounced floral character. The *brouillis* then goes on to the second distillation, the *bonne chauffe.* The residue of this distillation, the "tails," is put aside to be combined later with the "heads" in a new batch of wine to make another *première chauffe.* The distiller's art is to isolate the "heart" of the brandy from its "heads" and "tails." From this "heart" will come much of the particular cognac's distinctive characteristics. The spirit is at this stage about 70 percent alcohol, by rule no more than 72 percent. Time will reduce its potency. When it is sold, it will be near but not less than 40 percent alcohol. Nine liters of wine will have gone into the making of one liter of cognac.

The next critically important step is the aging process. Newly distilled cognac tastes raw and oily, displaying an unpleasant coppery flavor called *goût de cuivre.* New cognac is aged in oak barrels from Limousin in France. The wood that goes into these barrels is always split, never sawn, and no glue or nails are used. The transforming chemical process is the interchange between the wood and distillate produced by air seeping through the pores of the barrel. After a year, the brandy is moved from new barrels to old ones, in order to prevent absorption of too much tannin. Oxidation, the evaporation of alcohol through the pores of the barrel, softens the alcoholic proof and gives cognac its final bouquet and golden hue. During this aging process, the color of the cognac changes from clear to amber as a result of the tannin in the wood. The lignin adds a soupçon of vanilla and cinnamon to the taste.

Cognac Paradise

Producers keep an archive of their best and oldest cognacs, some a century old, in hermetically sealed glass demijohns in a special part of the cellar called the *paradis.*

Now the final, and perhaps the most difficult and complex, step of creating cognac takes place. Here is where the art of *le maître de chai,* the cellar master, comes into play: the *coupage,* or blending. The *maître de chai,* by blending together as many as fifty distillates with differing personalities and ages, from different growing areas, defines the style of the cognac. The blend is put into

After~Dinner Drinks

large casks, and, if necessary, distilled water or dilute brandy is added to bring the spirit down to shipping proof of 40 to 43 percent alcohol. Sometimes caramel is added for color and cane syrup to offset harshness. After the cognac is bottled, the French government awards the producer a certificate, the Acquit Régional Jaune d'Or, which guarantees that the brandy comes from Cognac.

Unlike wine, cognac does not carry vintage years or dates to assist the buyer in estimating its quality. Stars in the case of quality brandies and letters that stand for English words are used. (Three of the principal Cognac entrepreneurs came from England: Hennessy, Hine, and Martell.) The age of a cognac indicates the length of time it has spent in the cask, not the time passed since it was made. Three stars usually mean the cognac has spent two and one-half years in wood—the minimum necessary to obey the rules that govern its designation as cognac. The letters VS on the label mean Very Superior and indicate that it has been aged for four to seven years in the barrel. Very Superior Old Pale, VSOP, or Réserve, means aging of five to thirteen years. Pale means that no coloring matter has been added. Some first-rate cognacs are almost clear, the pale gold of an unaged spirit such as marc. Extra, XO, Napoléon, Vieille Réserve, or Hors d'Age all indicate an age of seven to forty years in wood. The longer the aging, the better the cognac— preferably twenty-five to forty years.

The dishes are cleared. The waiter hovers. Your party peruses an after-dinner drink list. Now is the time to savor an extraordinary cognac—perhaps it will be a Remy Martin XO Special Cognac Fine Champagne composed of 80 percent Grande Champagne and 20 percent Petite. It is served in a tulip-shaped glass or a small pear-shaped snifter. A century ago, it would have been served in a *ballon,* but modern tasters argue that the alcohol of the cognac concentrates in the neck of this large, balloon-shaped glass and rises straight to the nose like a sharp left jab. The tulipe, only 4 cm deep, will allow the aroma to reveal itself slowly, to display its

When in Paris

In France, cognac drinkers often order a *fine* ("Feen"). Hemingway's lost generation did just that in Paris. A *fine* is always a cognac; the word is just shorthand for Fine Champagne Cognac. It can be a blend of brandies from the districts of Grande Champagne and Petite Champagne, but it must contain at least 50 percent Grande.

subtle fragrance. You smell, gently. You examine the amber color. It should be lively, not dull. You swish the cognac, letting your hand warm it; this is called the "humanization" of the brandy. Then you apply the "second nose," discovering the full bouquet. And, finally, the moment of truth. You taste. All the receptors of your palate will be engaged: first sweetness, then saltiness, then bitterness, and, finally, acidity. The finish should be smooth, velvety—any burn or rawness would incriminate a cheap brandy. You detect a hint of vanilla, an oaky sweetness. The cognac taste leaves a deep impression, a lingering aftertaste. You find it good.

Some of the more widely distributed and popular cognacs are: A. Hardy, Courvoisier, Delamain, Hennessy, Hine, Jean Danflou, Martell, Remy Martin, and Salignac. The expert F. Paul Pacult gives his highest recommendation to Pierre Ferrand. Alas, he notes that Ferrand produces only eight hundred cases a year. Of one of its best cognacs, the Réserve Ancestrale Cognac Grande Champagne, only two hundred bottles are put onto the market each year.

*A*RMAG*N*AC

To the southeast of Cognac in the province of Gascony and the *département* of Gers is the home of foie gras, the Three Musketeers, and a brandy called Armagnac. (One of the Musketeers, d'Artagnan, was a real-life Gascon, who has named after him a recipe for roast capon with Armagnac in its sauce.) Armagnac has been made for five hundred years—two hundred more than cognac—and comes from the only other officially designated brandy region in France.

Despite Armagnac's longer history and its position in one of France's notable gustatory regions, it has been greatly overshadowed in the world's eye by cognac; its sales are around 6 percent of those of its more famous competitor by the Atlantic. The same grapes that are used for making cognac are the basis of Armagnac, the Ugni Blanc, Colombard, and Folle Blanche, with the preference steadily moving toward the higher-yielding Ugni Blanc. A few other varieties that grow well in the region, such as Jurançon, Meslier, and a hybrid called Baco 22a, are acceptable candidates for the alembic.

Armagnac is aged in oak, as is cognac, although Armagnac utilizes the tight-grained heartwood of black oak from France's Monlezun forest. The type of wood and the distillation process are important differences between Armagnac and cognac. Armagnac is distilled over low heat in a single, continuous process. Fans of Armagnac say this creates a brandy that preserves more of the character of the fruit and is more robust than cognac. Devotees of cognac argue the double distillation process produces a more elegant and complex brandy.

There are three districts that produce Armagnac: Bas-Armagnac, Ténarèze, and Haut-Armagnac. It is claimed that the heartiest, if not the best, Armagnac comes from the lower or Bas area. The Bureau National Interprofessionel de l'Armagnac establishes regulations for the production of this brandy. The aging requirements are similar to those of cognac, perhaps even longer. The same abbreviations to designate aging are used: VS (three to seven years), VO or VSOP (five to fifteen years), XO (six to forty years), and Hors d'Age (ten to fifty years). Another distinction made by Armagnac is the allowance of age statements on the label; the number must be the age of the youngest component of the blend.

Armagnac is generally stronger than cognac—about 110 proof. Those who prefer this brandy would argue that it is more flavorful. Indeed, descriptions by expert tasters such as F. Paul Pacult tantalize both in the range and

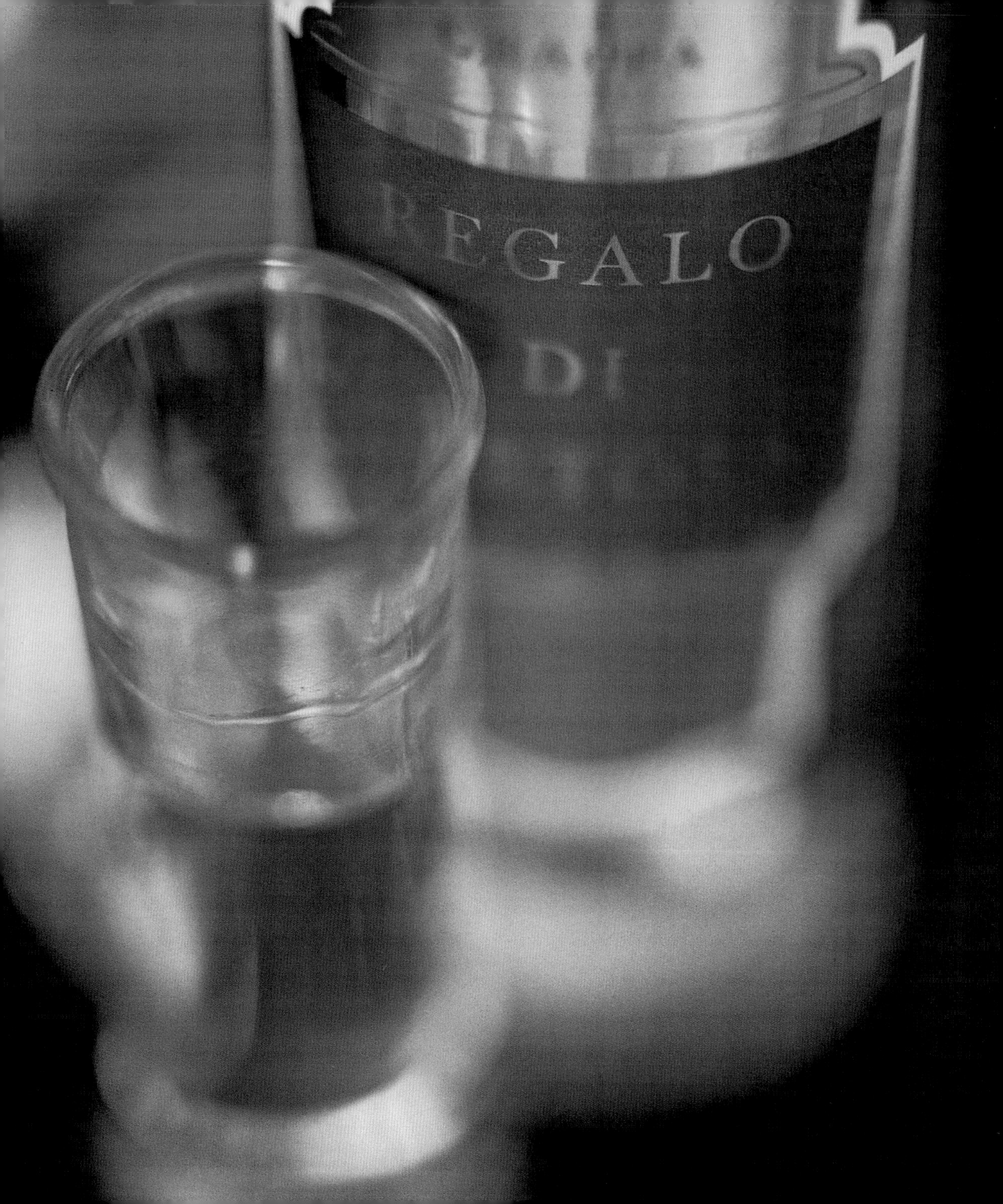
REGALO
DI

kind of flavor nuances to be found in the best Armagnacs. He describes the taste of the Cerbois 1962 Bas-Armagnac: "the vanilla/biscuity note opens shop in the second pass, developing into a dark toffee, maple, bacon-fat-like presence in the third nosing; ditto, the third pass . . . the flavors range from walnuts to maple to candied almonds."

Producers' names to look for when shopping for Armagnac are B. Gelas, Cerbois, Darroze, de Montal, Janneau, Laberdolive, Larressingle, Marquis de Caussade, Samalens, and Sempé. Sempé and Janneau seem to be more readily available on drink lists and in liquor stores. Remember that the words "Bas" and "Haut" on the labels refer to geography, not quality, and that in this case lower is better than higher.

My taste in spirits runs to dryness, strength, and uncomplicated flavors—probably I would be with the partisans of Armagnac, if I were ever forced to decide forever between the two brandies. It can be difficult to find, but it is well worth the effort.

Grappa

Of all the after-dinner drinks, grappa is the one that skyrocketed from what some may call a well-deserved obscurity not only to popularity but to *alto modo* and *molto expensivo.* Grappa was once a brutish liquor made from leftover wine debris, served in unlabeled bottles, rustic to a fault, straight from the still, corrosive, seemingly good only to see a poor Italian farmer through a long winter's night. Now it is sold in hand-blown bottles, inhabits the bar's top shelf, and sells for double figures by the shot. I have seen a list devoted entirely to grappa, domestic, imported, and in flights, which offers nearly fifty different brands and styles. (A flight is made up of four or five small samplings of the same beverage, each from a different producer.)

Pomace, the grape skins, pulp, seeds, and stems left behind from the making of wine, is the stuff of grappa. The pomace is pressed again, then the juice fermented and distilled into a spirit that at its best is the aromatic, transparent soul of the grape.

Lacking time in the barrel to color and soften (although some upscale grappas are now aged), grappa is more properly an eau de vie than a brandy. Grappas are not blended as are cognacs and Armagnacs, so the nature of the grape is important. For grappa fans, it is the taste of the fruit, as it is with eaux de vie, not the artistry of the *maître de chai,* that counts. Nebbiolo, Muscat, Pinot Noir, Merlot, Cabernet Sauvignon, Gavi, Barolo, Valpolicella, and Brunello are a few of the well-known varietal grapes that are the basis for the better grappas. The taste of grappa takes precedence over aroma; consequently, the choice of a glass is not as much of a consideration as with cognac. Some like grappa chilled and served in a martini glass; for most, a brandy pony glass or three-ounce snifter is more than satisfactory. Stemless, cylindrical glasses resembling Delmonico, or juice glasses, are also used to serve grappa and other eaux de vie.

Some of the makers' names to look for are: the AB Collection (named for Antonella Bocchino), Gaja, Jacapo Poli, Lungarotti, Michele Chiarlo, Nardini, Nonino, Ruffino, Susanna Gualco, and Tenuta Il Poggione.

Marc

Grappa has a French brother named Marc. He is not nearly as famous, and one would go through many American restaurants' after-dinner drink lists to find even one mention of him. However, in France, marc can be found on just about every restaurant and café list of drinks.

Marc is made the same way as grappa, from grape pomace, which is called *marc* in French. In France, the region determines the nature of the marc. The two principal marcs are the highly aromatic Marc de Champagne, using grape pomace from all the wines in that region, and Marc de Bourgogne, from Burgundy. A few estates offer marc that has been aged in oak. A third region, Alsace, also produces marc in some quantity.

It's powerful stuff, and would be an appropriate end to a meal hosted by Rabelais' Gargantua.

AMERICAN BRANDIES

Interestingly, America, mainly California, has a long and rather undistinguished—until recently—history of brandy-making. Undoubtedly, the friars made it in the days of the Spanish mission. In the late nineteenth century, unsold or unsellable wine was converted into saleable spirit. One notable owner of a vineyard whose wines were more readily marketable distilled than merely fermented was then-Governor Leland Stanford.

However, in the 1970s, several pioneers of fine brandy-making appeared on the California scene. They tried cognac-style grapes, used pot stills, double-distilled, and aged in charred oak barrels. Russell Woodbury used the Ugni Blanc grape, the same as is at the heart of much cognac. A division of Remy-Martin, RMS, distilled another cognac grape, the Colombard, which grew prolifically in California and was made into a popular sweetish white wine. Remy's current notable brandy comes from Carneros Alambic Distillery in the Napa Valley. Hubert Germain-Robin made a brandy from Gamay and Pinot Noir grapes, and today Germain-Robin is one the best and most interesting distillers of American brandy. F. Paul Pacult gives its Pinot Noir Single-Barrel Brandy five stars, the highest recommendation, and calls it the "greatest American grape-based brandy ever made."

"Be sometimes to your country true,
Have once the public good in view;

Bravely despise champagne at Court
And choose to dine at home with port."

—Jonathan Swift

FORTIFIED WINES

Port and its less familiar cousin Madeira are fortified wines, which means that during their wine-making process, fermentation is halted by the addition of brandy. Each is aged, sometimes for decades, and at its best, each becomes an after-dinner drink of richness and complexity.

Port

Just as newly invented champagne was the fancy French trend in Swift's time, port was British and homey, despite its Portuguese origins. Called "the Englishman's wine," it has been historically true if not politically correct that it was reserved only for men. Englishwomen drank sherry. Although port is enjoyed globally today, the British were its first appreciators and importers; they dominated the industry, as the house names of Warre, Sandeman, Cockburn, Graham's, and Taylor, Fladgate, and Yeatman attest. It has been said that the last outposts of the British Empire are the city of Oporto,

which gives the wine its name; Vila Nova de Gaia, the shipping center to the south; and the Douro valley, where the grapes are grown and trod. It's an irony Swift would have keenly appreciated.

The Portuguese drink lots of Portuguese wine—the pleasant *vinho verde* is popular in Oporto—but very little port. The ancient Portuguese, a Celtic tribe called the Lusitanians who lived in the region, made wine hundreds of years before Christ. But despite all the vinous history and consumption in Portugal, if the British had not fallen in love with port, it probably would never have been exported for the rest of the world to enjoy.

Any wine calling itself "Port"—or Porto—in England must come from the Douro Valley in Portugal. It is an inhospitable place, both to humans and plants, with stony soil, steep gorges, and a climate that swings from snow in the winter to searing heat in the summer. The Portuguese poet Miguel Torga wrote, "Man with his bare hands wrings wine from stone."

As befitting its *terroir*—the combination of geological, climatic, and vinicultural factors that create character in a wine grape—nothing about port is easy. It has a rich, knotty history, comes in many styles and kinds, and offers an uncommonly complicated system of classification and regulation. Port is categorized into five basic styles: vintage, ruby, tawny, single quinta, and white. Vintage port is considered to be the best. Made from wines of a single vintage that are bottled no later than two years after picking, vintage port is allowed to age for several decades. Ruby ports are aged in wood, sometimes for only two years, then bottled and are ready to drink. A combination of grapes from different years produces tawny port, which may then be aged for many years in wood and called "aged tawny port." A single vintage tawny is called a Colheita. Single quintas are high-quality vintage ports from the vineyards of one estate. White ports are, not surprisingly, composed of white grapes.

For this book, I will leave white port for a summer afternoon (an English pub favorite used to be "port and lemon," a combination of white port and fizzy lemonade) or an aperitif (the French especially favor it), and ruby port for those with a sweet tooth or insufficient funds for the real stuff. I will concentrate on vintage reds and aged tawnies, the ports traditionally served in the drawing room.

And, although several countries make perfectly fine port, the port discussed here is exclusively from Portugual.

Although port originated in Portugal, it started with the British. In 1678, the British, in continuing conflict with France, had placed an embargo on trade with that country. In their search for a new supply of wine, some merchants had brought in Portuguese red wine, but to the British palate it was thin and sour. The search went on for something heavier and sweeter. Two adventuresome English merchants allegedly pressed into the mountainous region of the Douro Valley in search of a more robust wine. They visited a monastery south of the Douro River where the abbot offered them a wine that was sturdier and smoother than any Portuguese red they had tasted. The abbot told them that brandy had been added to the wine during the fermentation process. In a slight variation on this story, the Englishmen found the wine at the monastery to their liking, and *they* added the brandy in order to protect it during its river journey to Oporto and shipment by sea to England. Either way, port was born.

In 1703, the future of port in England was assured. Queen Anne's war with France was on. The signing of the Methuen trade treaty lowered duty rates on Portuguese wines imported into England in exchange for like treatment of English textiles imported into Portugal. The sudden British taste for this wine, combined with attractive pricing and a singular, in fact exclusive, relationship between the supplier and the demander made port an enormous success for the next fifty years.

Then, as with cognac, the demand for the product led to imitation and adulteration. Demand dwindled for the unappetizing frauds on the market, even as their supply increased. The importation of port by England plummeted to almost zero. The winemakers of the Douro Valley appealed to the Marquis of Pombal, a state functionary who had been given almost absolute power because of his masterful handling of the aftermath of the Lisbon earthquake. He was the man in control of Portugal's wine industry. The marquis established a regulatory body — some say it was responsible for the first official demarcation in the wine world — that set port prices, mapped the Douro, rated the wines, and earmarked the best, which were made in the style the British preferred, for export to its biggest market in Europe.

During this time, another unusual phenomenon took place, again with the British involved. The British merchants established themselves in the region, first in the Douro, then the shippers set up headquarters in the port city of Oporto. Among the first of these companies, called lodges, were Taylor, Fladgate, Croft, and Warre. By the mid-1700s, England had become the biggest and most influential foreign trader in Portugal. The English insinuated themselves into Portuguese life and yet remained separate.

In 1790, a granite mansion called the Factory House was erected by a group of traders called the British Association. It continues to function both as a trade association and a club, one restricted to the British port firms, and is a symbol of this peculiar business, devoted both to the industry's bottom line and the quality of its product. At the weekly lunch, gentlemen are expected to wear jackets, even at the height of summer, and ladies are expected to lunch elsewhere. Every lunch offers a blind tasting of vintage ports, in which the diners try to identify the wine and its vintage year. Dinners are even more formal. As the meal is finished, the doors to an adjoining room are opened. Everyone rises, takes his napkin, and goes to a table in the second room. Away from food and the clutter of the dining table, by candlelight, the decanter of vintage port is circulated, clockwise, of course, as is the tradition.

It is generally agreed that the best port in the world comes from the upper reaches of the Douro Valley. The Douro River (River of Gold) runs from the Spanish border through the Serra do Marão mountains before emptying into the Atlantic at Oporto. It has carved out steep gorges and hillsides of slate and granite impossible for mules, much less tractors, to work. Its soil is poor and stony, fit only for scrub and the olive tree. The mountains separate this stretch of the valley from the rest of Portugal, in a climate of freezing

Port Tongs

Every port aficionado needs a pair of port tongs. The handles are like those of garden shears, but instead of blades, the implement has two semi-circular tongs, which when pressed together make a ring. If one is confronted by an ancient bottle of port and suspects that the cork might crumble under a corkscrew, the tongs can be employed. They are heated to red-hot and clasped around the neck of the bottle for a few moments, then released. The neck is wiped with a damp cloth, and—voilà!—cleanly severed from the bottle.

winters and baking summers. Below the thin topsoil, the slatelike schist has to be pulverized by hand or by dynamite in order for the vines to take hold. The growers cut terraces into the rock so that the rows of vines can be tended, even by hand. (Recently, new terraces called *patamares* have been made to accommodate small tractors, greatly improving the efficiency of the growers.)

The hardships facing the growers of the Douro Valley are precisely what makes port so distinctive. The granular soil allows the vines to penetrate deeply, a critical factor in the dry, torrid summers. The heat causes the grapes to ripen to an incredibly high sugar content, leading to a correspondingly high alcohol level during the fermentation process. Brandy must be added to stop the alcohol level of the grapes from becoming too high. Naturally sweet and strong before the addition of brandy, the port will age in casks and bottles to develop its elegant and unique flavor.

Port is a blended wine; more than one grape goes into each barrel. Almost fifty varieties are usable, and about twenty are officially approved by the port regulatory body. Touriga Naçional is considered the best, while other popular grapes are Tinta Roriz, Touriga Francesa, Tinta Barroca, and Tinta Cão. Each has its own characteristics, and responds to different growing conditions, but a combination of these grapes will supply the desired deep color, tannin, capacity for aging, and high sugar content. In the old days, rows of different vines were grown on one terrace, their fruit to be blended in the crushing process. Now different varieties are grown in blocks and vinified separately.

In September, itinerant pickers arrive in the Douro. Harvesting begins at dawn, when the *rogas,* or pickers, head to the vineyards, often singing to the accompaniment of a drum or accordion. At night, the crush begins. Robert Finigan observed that the "human foot is the perfect tool for extracting juice from grapes, as the ancients knew," and that tool is still used in the making of port. The pickers, in shorts, climb into large granite troughs and begin walking in place, with grapes rising to their thighs. The foreman beats a drum and chants out the march, *"um-dois"* ("one-two"). Port and brandy are available to fuel the effort. As fewer people are willing to do this kind of work, producers are turning to mechanical presses and pumps to do the fermentation process. Unfortunately, the constant yet gentle pressing provided by the human foot is superior in extracting the color from the skins, which are discarded before brandy is added. The best ports are still made by foot.

Fermentation is monitored closely by the winemaker, and when the time is right, neutral grape brandy is added to the partially fermented wine in a ratio of one to five to kill the fermenting yeasts and stabilize the liquid. This young port is a combination of rough, tannic, sweet wine and equally rough spirit. The mixture is transported to Oporto by truck. When the wines are in the lodges, they are evaluated by character and potential and separated into *lotes,* lots, for aging in barrels of old oak; new wood is not used because it would impart a vanilla flavor to the port. Aging takes place in the lodges of the major port firms in Vila Nova de Gaia, across the mouth of the Douro from Oporto. The best port takes two to three decades.

The process of aging and choosing a vessel for the different styles of port is complicated. The only common denominator is that all port begins to age in casks; then, depending on the lodge's estimate of the wine's quality, it could be sent to market, continue to age in wood, or be transferred to the bottle.

The better ports are either cask-aged or bottle-aged. Tawnies are aged in wood; vintage ports, after a brief stay in the barrel, age in the bottle. But, as I said, the system is complicated. Port has been called "hierarchical" because there is a style for everyone. Farther up the hierarchy are two styles of tawny. One is aged in wood for ten to forty years, then bottled and sold; it is called an "indicated age tawny." The other is called "aged tawny port," blended from only one vintage, aged for a minimum of seven years and as much as forty in wood, and then bottled. The label will state the vintage and bottling date. One of these tawnies, called Colheita, is much sought after by discriminating port drinkers. Some experts feel a superb "aged tawny" to be equal to a vintage.

On to the dark, rich ports—the ones we think of when we conjure up the after-dinner retreat to the drawing room or library, a fire burning, a bowl of walnuts and a chunk of Stilton, maybe a cigar. The drinker—a stout, satisfied patrician, leg up, foot swaddled—suffers from a touch of gout. There are four styles of fine red port: crusted, late-bottled vintage, single-quinta vintage, and, the crown jewel, vintage.

The
Port Label

Choosing a bottle of port can be one of the labors of Hercules. The label can help. All premium ports have labels that indicate what style it is and how it was made. You should be able to find the following information.

If you want a port from Portugal look for the word *Porto*. It means authentic port. The name Port with a capital *P* is protected in the United Kingdom and designates Portugal as the origin.

The producer's name should be on the label, which will further confirm provenance. A few well-known and estimable shippers are: A. A. Ferreira; Adriano Ramos Pinto; Cockburn; Fonseca; Sandeman; Silva & Cosens; Taylor, Fladgate, and Yeatman; and Warre.

Remember, there are four basic styles: white, ruby, tawny, and vintage. White and ruby are clearly marked. Vintage port labels will always indicate the vintage year, the year bottled, the shipper, and the designation "Vintage Port." Tawnies are not always labeled as such, but statements of age such as "10 Years" or "20 Years" mean the port is an aged tawny. Late-bottled vintages are so described or by the abbreviation LBV. If the port has been produced from grapes grown on one farm or estate, the word "quinta" should appear on the label.

The word "reserve" is frequently and imprecisely used by the port trade and can cause confusion. There is no substitute for a knowledgeable wine merchant when investing in a quality port.

Crusted port is not commonly found these days. Not recognized by the regulatory body in Oporto, it had been previously bottled by merchants in the United Kingdom. Now, by Portuguese law, all Portuguese port must be bottled indigenously, so the future of crusted seems dim. A blend of several vintages, it has been aged in wood for three to four years, bottled, and then matured further for a minimum of two years. Unfiltered, it develops a substantial amount of sediment and must be decanted carefully. It brings to mind romantic images of the lit candle, the careful pouring from bottle to decanter, and the port tongs.

Late-bottled vintage is a blending of wines from a single vintage, aged in wood for four to six years and then bottled ready to drink. It does not age further. One expert has suggested that this style of port was intended to be a poor man's version of vintage. Others feel it can be a good value.

The top rungs of the Hierarchy are occupied by single-quinta vintage and vintage. The former is a high-quality wine from one farm—port's equivalent of "estate-bottled wine"—that has been aged for two years in wood, then bottled and left to mature for five to fifty years. The best can be compared with vintage.

Vintage port is the port of legend, the port that the wealthy lay down for their sons or grandsons, expecting that it will have matured by the time their offspring reach their majority. (Traditionally, the bottled contents of a barrel—approximately 145 gallons—were laid down for the lucky little fellow's cellar.) Aged in wood for two years, it is then bottled and matured for five to fifty years. On average, only 3 percent of Portugal's annual port production becomes vintage. Only the best vineyards and the best wines from the best vintages are put aside for vintage port and "declared." Exceptionally full and fruity with enormous levels of tannin, the cream of vintage will not reach its peak for 20 years. Some require 50 to 60 years. It is this wine that makes a shipper's reputation. Vintage port is not produced every year. Only when all the factors are right will a shipper declare a vintage, and that after eighteen months or so of consideration and evaluation. According to one expert, there have been only seven "peerless, five-star legends" in the twentieth century.

Every several years, usually no more than three per decade among the better houses, a port shipper will "declare" a vintage port. Not all choose the same year; the decision comes after a year and a half of thinking, tasting, consulting, and planning. It is a decision that lasts the lifetime of those making it. Not every shipper declares in the same year, although in the years when the sun and the rain and other factors of the *terroir* cohere on behalf of the grape, inevitably a large number of houses declare. Each house makes its own decision (although the declaration must be ratified by the Instituto do Vinho do Porto, the regulatory body). Then the house must shape the wine, a blend of several varieties and several estates from the same vintage. Each shipper or house has a style, and its vintage develops its own unique flavor. The great years of this century are thought to be 1908, 1927, 1935, 1945, 1963 (which probably won't reach its peak until the millennium), 1977, 1983, and 1985. Recently, 1991 was declared by most shippers, and 1995 is said to have monumental potential.

As might be expected, vintage ports ready to drink are hard to come by and quite expensive. However, one interested in tasting more than the common ports widely available might seek out an aged tawny or a late-bottled vintage or sample the selection offered by a fine restaurant. If one is lucky or rich enough to have a cellar and collects vintage port to lay down, a few rules apply. A proper cellar, however small, will be cool and dark and free from vibrations. The temperature should be consistent. Bottles should be placed on their sides, with the label up for the length of storage, so that sediment will be deposited on the opposite side. This will aid in decanting. When the day (or year) comes to enjoy the port, it needs to stand upright for twenty-four hours so the sediment falls to the bottom. The bottle neck is wiped clean and the cork removed, and then the wine is slowly but continuously poured into another vessel—usually an attractive decanter. Sometimes a funnel is used. A lit candle or other light source behind the bottle will reveal when the sediment reaches the neck of the bottle and the decanting process ends. Port should be served in clean, clear glasses such as the small Paris goblet, the four-and-one-half-ounce savoy glass, or the taller, tulip-shaped ISO (International Standards Organization) tasting glass, and poured to no more than two-thirds full.

The moment of truth. The tasting. As with wine and cognac, three senses are brought into play: sight, smell, and taste. Ports come in many colors, even those of a single style; whatever the hue, the wine should be bright and uncloudy. The wine is swirled and smelled. Its nose should be rich and full, fruity for reds and nutty for tawnies. On the palate the port should offer more complex properties and flavors. Usually sweetness is tasted first, then acidity. Some of the flavors that expert tasters detect in red ports are blackberry, black cherry, black fruits in general, chocolate, tobacco, and raisins; and in tawnies, coffee, toffee, cashews, almonds, and tropical fruit.

The company is convivial. The port is first-rate, say, a Quinta Do Noval 20-Year-Old Tawny Porto. Remember the British tradition. After serving your neighbor on the right, then yourself, you start the decanter on its way clockwise. It stalls in conversation halfway down the table. No need for alarm. Just request "the bishop," and the laggard decanter should be on its way around the table.

MADEIRA

With its close relation, port, the fortified wine Madeira shares a similar unusual history. Undiscovered and uninhabited until 1418 or 1420, the island of Madeira is a small, mountainous tropical island about four hundred miles off the coast of Morocco. When João Gonçalves, a captain of Prince Henry the Navigator, founded a settlement on the Bay of Funchal, the island was densely wooded. The Captain of Madeira, as Gonçalves was known, burned down the forests—the fire was said to have lasted for seven years. Where the Douro Valley is harsh, Madeira is lush. The combination of volcanic soil, the potash from the fire, and centuries of organic matter from the forest made the island especially fertile. The export of wine and sugarcane, and later, bananas, created a rich colony for Portugal.

Madeira was a more popular drink hundreds of years ago than now; its success was due as much to politics as taste. By the sixteenth century, Madeira—mostly a robust wine made from the Malvasia

grape—was being exported to Europe. But it was colonial America that became the biggest fan of the wine. It was said to be George Washington's favorite drink, and Thomas Jefferson toasted the completion of the Declaration of Independence with a tot of Madeira. Its popularity among the revolutionaries was due in large part to the mother country's omission of the island of Madeira from the onerous tariffs levied on the colony's imports. American and British ships sailing to America stopped at Madeira for water and supplies and took on a few pipes (145-gallon barrels) of the wine. Madeira remained fashionable until vineyards throughout Europe were devastated by phylloxera and oidium, a powdery mildew. Although you will find Madeira on fine restaurant after-dinner drink lists, its popularity in the United States is nothing like it was in the eighteenth and nineteenth centuries.

Madeira shares with port the distinction of being fortified with grape brandy. It is the only wine that improves when it is heated. In earlier times, casks of the wine were sent on long sea voyages, inevitably passing through the tropics, to the New World. This traveling wine, known as *vinho da roda,* wine of the round voyage, baked under the tropical sun. Amazingly, this heating process, called "maderization" and considered a great flaw in white table wines, gave the wine a delicious, nutty, caramel-toffee, burnt quality. In the eighteenth century, Madeira makers discovered that adding grape brandy during the fermentation process, as with port, resulted in an even more luscious wine. Now, the conditions of the torrid sea voyages are recreated in the form of *estufas,* hot rooms or tanks lined with hot water pipes, where the wine "cooks" for three to six months at temperatures between 95 and 120 degrees Fahrenheit.

The principal grapes that go into Madeira are the Malvasia Candiae (also known as Malmsey, an ancient grape originally from Crete); the Sercial (a Riesling); Verdelho; Bual or Boal; and the Tinta Negra Mole, used as a blend. The Sercial and Verdelho make drier, all-purpose wines, while the sweeter Bual and the

Wine in a Cradle

It was believed that in addition to the heat of the sea voyage, the motion of the ship contributed to the special maturation of Madeira. Famous shipping families in America used to put a cask of Madeira in a cradle at the entrance of their offices. Everyone who came to call was expected to give the cradle a push. In this way, the wine was kept endlessly rocking all the working day.

mahogany Malmsey are definitely for dessert wines.

As with port, much of the vineyard work on Madeira is done by hand. Madeira vines are not attentively pruned; they grow luxuriantly in the tropical climate and rich irrigated soil on trellises, with vines twenty feet long.

Merchants and shippers buy while the grapes are still on the vine. They supervise the ripening and picking process, often demanding that pickers return to the vineyards three or four times to ensure harvesting only the ripest grapes. The juice ferments for two to four weeks and then grape brandy is added, killing the yeasts. At this stage, the wine is called Vinho Claro.

After the wine is cooked in the *estufas,* it is known as Vinho Estufado. Then it rests and is racked into fresh barrels. It is now Vinho Trasfugado. Finally, an additional hit of brandy brings the wine up to an alcohol level of around 20 percent, and it is known as Vinho Generoso. It is then blended with similar wines and matured for years.

Madeira is among the longest lived of wines. After phylloxera destroyed vineyards little more than a century ago, the vintage wines were mixed with newer, younger plantings, so it is difficult to estimate how long a great Madeira could live. In the last decade or so, prize bottles such as an 1891 Bual and an 1885 Malmsey have been offered for sale.

As with port and cognac, Madeira is categorized according to age. Premium Madeiras usually begin with the Five-Year-Old Reserve; the primary grape variety is displayed on the label. Moving up the scale are Ten-Year-Old and Fifteen-Year-Old Reserves and Fresquiera Twenty-Year-Old. All vintage Madeiras must come from one of the noble grape varieties and be matured in oak casks for at least twenty years plus two years in the bottle before being offered to the public.

Some of the more important shippers are Blandy's, Cossarts, Justino Henriques, and Leacock's. F. Paul Pacult recommends Blandy's Malmsey Ten-Year-Old, Cossarts Duo Centenary Celebration Bual, Henriques Verdelho 1934, and Leacock's Bual Ten-Year Old. Madeira is served in the same glassware as port. Some of the tastes that recur in fine Madeiras are coffee, chocolate, caramel, almonds, and dark fruits and berries. Although a Madeira could be paired with dessert, its richness and sweetness qualify it as a dessert itself.

dESSERT WINES

"Dessert wines" are a catchall category, encompassing a great many varieties of grapes, individual styles, and means of vinification. In principle, they include port and Madeira. The qualifier "dessert" is a bit of a paradox. Many devotees of these wines recommend they be drunk following dessert or as dessert; others that they accompany dessert. They can do both. They have sweetness in common. They are an after-dinner drink, whether with dessert or as a finale. They can be lumped together and called "sweet wines."

Sweet wines—if we exclude fortified wines that have been strengthened by the addition of a spirit—are made in such a way as to concentrate the amount of sugar in the grape, which in combination with the alcohol produced by the concentration inhibits the action of the yeast. All begin by being processed after the harvest time of other grapes, hence their other designation, "late-harvest wines." Three basic techniques are employed to make the wines: leaving the grapes on the vines

Vinum Classicus

Dried-grape wines have an incredibly long and rich history. They are the wines of the ancient and classical worlds. Hesiod, in the eighth century B.C., wrote about wine made from dried grapes in his *Works and Days*. These are the wines of Homer, the most famous being made in the Greek islands. Later, dried-grape wines were traded widely thoughout the Mediterranean at the time of the Greek city-states. The Phoenicians exported wine from Lebanon to North Africa, Spain, Sicily, Sardinia, and Carthage. Because of their robustness, these wines were able to "travel" at a time when stoppered bottles were unknown. The Romans continued the tradition. Writers such as Cato, Pliny, Horace, and Virgil provide us with details of this tradition of winemaking. Unhappily, Greece has just about given up the tradition, although it survives in France, Hungary, and a few other European countries. Italy is the principal carrier of the torch, Vin Santo being the best-known example.

to shrivel or start to raisin; allowing the grapes to freeze on the vine; or allowing the grapes to become infected by the noble rot, *Botrytis cinerea.* Each technique concentrates flavors and sugars while keeping acid levels high, which prevents overpowering sweetness.

Drying the grapes—or partially raisining them—is the simplest and oldest technique for making sweet wines. In ancient times, the stems of grape bunches were twisted to block the flow of sap to the berry. Then the grapes could dry on the vine. Other techniques include just leaving them to dry like raisins by putting them on mats of straw or reed or on racks of bamboo; sometimes the vines are hung in sheds over a long period of alternating heat and cold.

Today, dried grapes are picked by experienced workers who choose only the best fruit. The bunches are arranged *spargolo,* loose, so that air can circulate around each grape. There is a direct relation between loss of water and concentration of sugar. Loss of water by evaporation may vary between 10 and 60 percent, but most winemakers aim for 35 to 40 percent. Pressing is gentle, and fermentation slow. The final product may be one of two styles: the first, in which the primary aromas are retained; and the second, in which these aromas are not encouraged in favor of a more complex bouquet. The former style is utililized with aromatic grapes such as Muscat and Riesling, where the hallmark of the style is fruitiness. The second is more complex, aged longer, and more traditional. Vin Santo and Valpolicella Amarone are examples.

Ice wine—called *Eiswein* in Germany and *vin de glace* in France—is made from frozen grapes, often not until December and January, picked early in the morning and pressed immediately so that water, in the form of ice crystals, is expelled and only the sweetest grape juice is left. When they are picked, they cannot have any form of rot, noble or otherwise, nor can they have any breaks in the skin. Ice wine is eminently drinkable when young, with a refreshing level of acidity. This late-harvest wine is a recent development, and a receptive market for it is being established. If the weather cooperates, it is much more economical to make than the risky botrytized wines, and more grapes are being devoted to this wine. (Some less successful ice wines are created by an artificial process known as cryoextraction.)

Noble rot. Botrytis bunch rot. In Latin, *Botrytis cinerea.* In French, *pourriture noble.* In German, *Edelfäule.* In Italian, *muffa nobile.* In Hungarian, *aszú.* Late in the growing season, given the right meteorological circumstances, a benevolent fungus may infect healthy, ripe white grapes and transform them into disgusting-looking fruit that can be made into the world's most superb and longest-living sweet wine. Warm sunny fall afternoons preceded by cool early morning mists are ideal for the appearance of the noble rot. But there is a Mr. Hyde side to this fungus, called gray rot, which is devastating when the weather is humid and the grapes are unripe or damaged. (If the grapes are healthy, the weather hot and dry without

No one knows exactly when winemakers discovered the benefits of noble rot, but it most certainly was by accident. Three locations that still produce botrytized wines figure in stories about the fungus. All are wine-growing areas with climate suitable for the mold.

In the Tokay region of Hungary, around 1650, it is said that a priest winemaker delayed his harvest because he feared an imminent attack by the Turks. No Turks showed, but the harvest was late, and the grapes covered by fungus. About to write off that year's vintage, he tasted the juice from one of the shriveled grapes. It was sweet and thick. He decided to make wine from the sad-looking fruit.

moisture, the noble Dr. Jekyll will ply his trade elsewhere, and the grapes will just build up sugar and become candidates for the sweet wines described above.)

What happens to the grape when penetrated by noble rot is chemically complex, making a grape juice that is entirely different from what would have been harvested normally, and not attributable just to elevated levels of sugar. The infected grape develops tiny brown spots, which actually protect the skin from other pests. The fungus reduces the water content of the grapes and consumes both sugar and acids. The result is an increase of the overall sugar content as the quantity of juice decreases. The grapes change color, ultimately to brown, as they dehydrate, and appear to be covered with a fine powder or ash (hence the description *cinerea*). The mysterious part of the process is the production of what has been described as an antibiotic, called "botryticine," which inhibits the fermentation, producing a wine that is sweet but uncommonly light. Honey is the flavor most associated with nobly rotten wine, and the miracle the botrytis fungus performs is no less than that of the honey bee.

Botrytized wines are both risky and costly to make, hence their great expense to the buyer. The climate and geography must be just right—cool, foggy mornings and sunny afternoons in autumn—and the grapes must be mature, healthy, and light-skinned. The grapes must be picked by hand when the rot is at its most beneficial. Many pickings take place over a period of weeks, even months. Several pressings may be required to get the dehydrated grapes to release any juice. Fermentation is necessarily slow because the yeasts are inhibited by the high sugar content and the botryticine. But when the wine is ready, it can age in the bottle for decades. The commonly used grapes for botrytized wines are Sémillon and Sauvignon Blanc, Riesling, Chenin Blanc, Gewürtztraminer, and Furmint.

There is a fourth category of dessert wine, Muscat, that should be mentioned. It might have been included in the company of port and Madeira, because some Muscats are lightly fortified (a process called *mutage* in France) with grape spirit. But in strength, style, and appeal, it seems properly a dessert wine. Probably the oldest variety of wine grape in the world, the Muscat produces a sweet wine with plenty of aroma, spice, and a musky taste. The muscatel of years past was rightly reviled, on a par with the infamous Thunderbird. But fine dessert Muscats are being produced, and I shall mention a few below.

There is no one glass one must use for sweet wines. The only rule is not to use a glass so small the serving, usually two ounces, reaches the brim. A small Paris goblet or a tulipe is fine, as is any glass suitable for port. The *copita,* in which sherry is served, is suitable.

What follows is a survey, by country, of some dessert wines. It intends to be neither exclusive nor inclusive. Many fine sweet wines are artisan creations and available readily only in their own locale. And, as with port, there are myriad sweet wines that have been industrially manufactured carrying the name Sauternes, Muscatel, or the like. But they are a drink, whether before, after, or instead of dinner, that only a wino could love.

(Origins of the Noble Rot continued)
Voilà (or the Hungarian equivalent)! Tokay was born.

In the Rheingau of Germany, the Schloss Johannisberg claims that in 1775 the harvest messenger bearing permission from the absentee-owner, the prince of Fulda, to pick the grapes got lost. When he found his way, the grapes had succumbed to the rot. The result of vinification was Germany's first botrytized *Spätlese.*

Sweet wines from the Loire and Bordeaux were in demand during the Middle Ages, but it is unlikely the noble rot was involved. More likely is the story that the effects of botrytis were discovered in 1847. Guess where? Château d'Yquem. And it has been making the world's most desirable sweet wine — Sauternes — ever since.

"ASHER & ADAMS EUROPE" (RARE EDITION WITH: "ALT PRUSSEN GRENZ"), DETAIL, PUB. 1876 BY ASHER & ADAMS IN WASHINGTON (COURTESY W. GRAHAM ARADER III GALLERY, SAN FRANCISCO).

ITALY

MALVASIA DELLE LIPARI. This wine made from dried grapes (*passito*) is sometimes lightly fortified (*liquoroso*). This ancient grape is much like the Muscat, spicy and distinctively orange in flavor. It hails from the volcanic island of Lipari off the coast of Sicily. The name comes from a corruption of Monemvasia, a busy Greek port in the Middle Ages, which was the shipping point for the popular sweet wine from the eastern Mediterranean. The word, further corrupted, became the Englishman's Malmsey. Many Malvasias are made today in different parts of Italy.

RECIOTO DI SOAVE. *Recioto* is a variant of *recie,* a northern Italian dialect term for ear. It gets its name because the ripest grapes are near the upper bunches, closer to the sun, sticking out like ears. The grapes, infected by the noble rot, are dried to raisins on wicker racks for several months before pressing and fermentation into a sweet white wine with about 14 percent alcohol.

AMARONE. This may be the most famous of Italy's dried-grape wines. It has also been known as Recioto della Valpolicella Amarone after its grape variety. It is made in the same way as *recioto,* although the drying period is

often longer, and it is aged in oak for as long as five years. The result is a powerful red wine, reaching 15 percent alcohol (30 proof). Although fans would have it accompany game and heavy meat dishes, it can be savored after dinner, in the manner of port.

VIN SANTO. The "holy wine," although at least one wine writer prefers the "wine of health." It comes from Tuscany, and is the region's classic dessert wine. A story has it that the wine was once dry and made sweet so children could sip it during Mass (and, one assumes, present the appearance at least of quiet devotion). It is made from Trebbiano, Canaiolo, and Malvasia—and in the past red Sangiovese—grapes carefully picked and dried on straw mats following harvest and then aged in oak. Vin Santo ranges in style from dry to super-sweet. Just about every vineyard in the region makes a batch of the wine. It is traditionally served to guests, along with dipping *biscotti,* called *cantucci* in Tuscany. The best Vin Santo can be expensive. Two producers to look for are Frescobaldi and Tenuta Trerose.

FRANCE

The winemakers in the Graves district of France's Bordeaux region produce some of the world's greatest sweet wines. Remarkably, they dedicate themselves exclusively to the task. Botrytis-affected wine is the rule, not the exception, as it is for other winemakers in Europe and California. Two of five communes in the Graves district are of particular interest: Sauternes and Barsac, which may be sold under its own appellation or as Sauternes.

SAUTERNES. Sémillon is the most important grape that goes into Sauternes. It is especially susceptible to the noble rot. Sauvignon Blanc gives the wine acidity that plays off the richer character of Sémillon. And, when used, the Muscadelle grape lends aroma. Sémillon, however, accounts for 80 percent of the mix of varieties planted in a Sauternes vineyard.

It has been said before: as with wine and real estate, location is everything. Or *terroir* and mesoclimate, that mystical potion of physical environment that the grape is brewed in. Sauternes has two rivers, the warm tidal Garonne and the cool, spring-fed Ciron, that flow into it. In the autumn their confluence encourages misty evenings that last until the late morning sun, the perfect weather for *Botrytis cinerea*. Moisture acitivates the fungus, and sunshine accelerates dessication. This process is a gift of nature, and transcends man's will and hand. Occasionally, the rot fails to develop or shows up so late in the year that rain and frost destroy the crop. There are vintages that do not result in wine. The patient acceptance of this risk makes Sauternes costly to produce. But when the fungus arrives and conditions are right, the grapes are selectively picked over a period of many weeks, usually the Sauvignon first, then the Sémillon. The careful sorting of the nobly rotten grapes from those with gray rot is appropriately called *triage*.

Château d'Yquem is rightly the most famous—and expensive—Sauternes. Many consider it to be the finest dessert wine in the world. When Sauternes was classified in 1855, Château d'Yquem was the only producer designated Premier Grand cru (the most superior vineyard). Recent great vintages are 1983, 1986, 1988, 1989, and 1990. The Château's *terroir* and commitment to quality are unparalleled. It takes an entire grape plant to produce one glass of wine.

Sauternes is often described as a nectar. It is a "fat" wine, with flavors of roasted nuts, honey, citrus, and tropical fruit, and redolent of flowers. Gourmands like to pair it with fois gras. That gives me a shiver—what the French call *de trop.*

A cautionary note: never, never, engage a Sauterne without the ultimate "s." As at the Teddy Bears' picnic, you'll be in for a big surprise.

BARSAC. Similar in taste to Château d'Yquem, Barsac is an elegant sweet wine. Barsac makes a wine lighter in body than its world-renowned neighbor Sauternes because of a different proportion of gravel, sand, and clay, and the presence of limestone in the soil. It and wines from other Sauternes region communes are delicious and kinder to the pocketbook than Château d'Yquem. Try a 1990 Doisy-Vedrines or an 1988, 1989, or 1990 Chateau Coutet.

MUSCAT DE BEAUMES-DE-VENISE. This *vin doux naturel,* naturally sweet fortified wine, comes from the southern Rhône region of France. It is made from the Muscat Blanc grape and lightly fortified, producing a golden sweet wine with the aroma of peaches and orange blossoms. Paul Jaboulet Aîné or Domaine de Coyeux are producers to look for.

The French sweet Muscats come from a variety of Muscat grapes. Heavily perfumed, they are *musque,* or musky. One theory has it that these redolent grapes attracted flies and were named for *musca,* the Latin word for the pesky insects. The oldest and noblest variety of this ancient grape is the Muscat Blanc à Petits Grains, which carries the defining muscat flavors of spice and orange flowers. Some other Muscats to look for are Muscat de Frontignan, Muscat de Lunel, and Muscat de Rivesaltes.

VIN DE PAILLE. "Straw wine" is a specialty of the Jura region. The grapes are dried on straw mats, and the dark dessert wine has the aroma and taste of dried fruit and nuts. This is a rare and expensive wine.

JURAÇON. This sweet wine from the Pyrenees is made from small yields of late-harvest Petite Manseng grapes that have been dried on the vines by the sun (*passerillage*). It tastes of honey, spices, and pineapple. It is claimed that in 1553 in his baptism as an infant, Henri IV's lips were moistened with the wine and that vinous drop inspired his later achievements.

MAS AMIEL MAURY. This *doux naturel* is made from the Grenache Noir grape. It spends at least a year in a *bonbonne,* a large glass jar or carboy, and then six, ten, or fifteen years in oak. It is quite comparable to a fine tawny port.

MONBAZILLAC. From southwest France, this is a botrytis-affected wine, made from the same grapes as Sauternes, but costing much less. Monbazillac is usually drunk after aging a few years, but some have improved for as many as twenty years.

VENDANGE TARDIVE AND SÉLECTION DE GRAINS NOBLES. These styles of sweet wines are made in Alsace. The former translates as "late harvest" and the latter, "selection of noble grapes," which means they have been infected by the noble rot.

GERMANY

Germany's laws regarding wines and labeling are not, like those of the French, based on soil, history, or vineyard distinctions, but simply on the degree of the grape's ripeness when picked and the sugar content of the grape juice. Qualitatswein mit Pradikat (QmP), quality wine with special distinctions, is the top rank in the German classification system that was adopted in 1971. Within this designation are six categories of sugar levels or ripeness. In order to identify that category on the label, the winemaker must be able to show that the legal standard for that class has been met. Sweet wines fall into five of the six classes, from the lowest sugar content to the highest. Prices also rise with sugar content. Austria also produces wines that are characterized by the same designations (plus a few more), but an enormous scandal in 1985 that involved adulteration of wine with diethylene glycol, a sweetening agent, soured many importers' enthusiasm for Austrian sweet wines.

SPÄTLESE, late picked or late harvest, should not be confused with the term when used in the United States. Some of these wines can be dry and matched with food, and others can be sweet.

AUSLESE, selected harvest, are sweet wines from grapes that have been chosen because they are especially ripe or carry *Edelfäule,* the noble rot. They are usually intense in perfume and flavor.

BEERENAUSLESE (the longer German terms often get abbreviated; this is referred to as BA), "selected berries," indicates that pickers selected by hand only overripe grapes showing signs of the noble rot. BA can be quite rare; in some years none is produced, and consequently what there is of it can be very expensive. Riesling and Huxelrebe are the typical grapes that go into BA. When it can be found, this deep golden wine is especially rich and luscious. The taste has compared to that of honey-soaked raisins.

EISWEIN, ice wine, is a German specialty, although it is now made in a few other countries, including the United States, Canada, and Austria. Demand for this sweet wine is a relatively new phenomenon; the 1962 vintage in Germany was the first to receive wide recognition and acclaim. Eiswein can be drunk young, and its high acidity is refreshing. Ironically, premium ice wines command higher prices than botrytized wines such as *Auslese* because their sugar content compares with that of a *Beerenauslese.*

TROCKENBEERENAUSLESE (or, for those short of breath, TBA), "selected dried berries," is the rarest and ripest of wines. It indicates berries or grapes that have been covered by the noble fungus and shriveled to raisins on the vine. Many vintages do not produce a drop of TBA, losing the grapes to rain, wind, hail, frost, animals, gray rot, or dehydration so severe there is no juice to press. The sugar level of the grape at this rank in the classification is actually higher than that of Sauternes, despite the colder climate. TBA is incredibly rich, usually a profound golden orange color, more appropriately called a nectar than a wine, the essence of the grape variety. Unsurprisingly, these wines fetch a handsome price.

HUNGARY

Tokay, or Tokaji, when produced in its nobly rotten style, is Hungary's best-known wine. Sweet Tokay was at one time extremely desirable in Europe, particularly at the French and Russian court during the eighteenth century. It became known as "the wine of kings and the king of wines."

Sheltered by the Carpathian Mountains from the east, west, and north, and home to two rivers, the region has the perfect climate of moist nights and warm days in the fall for the noble rot, called *aszú.* The principal grape is the spicy Furmint, mixed with the aromatic Harslevelu, and sometimes with a bit of Yellow Muscat for softness. (These three grapes play the same roles in Tokay as Sémillon, Sauvignon Blanc, and Muscadelle do in Sauternes.)

The making of Tokay has one quite important and interesting difference from that of other botrytized wines. The shriveled grapes are mashed into a sweet paste and stored in small barrels called *puttonyos.* This paste is added to a base wine made from unaffected grapes in a larger cask called a *gönci.* The more *puttonyos* put into a *gönci,* the sweeter the wine. The result is matured in wood for four to eight years. Another curious feature of Tokay are the caves, tunnels really, cut into hillsides (supposedly to protect the wine from those troublesome Turks of old). The walls are covered by a thick black fungus that forms yeasts on the surface of the wine, similar to the situation in which *flor* forms on sherry in Jerez. This adds a distinct flavor to the wine.

Tokays range in sweetness, according to Hungarian standards, from three *puttonyos* to six. Surpassing all is Essenciat, which at eight *puttonyos* may be the sweetest and longest-lived wine in the world. The sugar content is so high that it ferments extremely slowly and is drinkable for perhaps as long as a century.

For an after-dinner treat, try Tokay labeled Tokaji Aszú. It should have the aroma and taste of apricots and of almonds in the older wines.

North America

Despite the absence of Europe's long tradition of making fine sweet wines, America today supports hundreds of makers of dessert wines. These wine entrepreneurs use all the natural forces at their disposal: the noble rot, ice, and sun. Most do their work in California, Washington, and British Columbia, but "late-harvest wines," the preferred denomination, are made in many states. Even the range of grape varieties used shows the entrepreneurs' spirit: Sauvignon Blanc; Sémillon; several kinds of Riesling; Gewürztraminer; several colors of Muscat; the German grapes Optima, Bacchus, and the hybrid Vidal Blanc (for ice wines); and even the lowly Zinfandel.

Following is just a small taste of the geographical range and stylistic variety of North America's late-harvest wines, listed by producer, with apologies to the other fine winemakers too numerous to include.

APEX in Washington State makes an ice wine from Gewürztraminer.

BERINGER, a well-known winemaker in California, offers a late-harvest wine made from Sauvignon Blanc and Sémillon grapes called "Nightingale."

CHATEAU STE. MICHELLE in the state of Washington makes an ice wine from Riesling grapes.

FAR NIENTE in California produces a sweet wine form Sémillon grapes called "Dolce."

J. LOHR, also in California, calls its sweet Riesling "Late Harvest."

HERMANN J. WIEMER VINEYARD in Finger Lakes, New York, uses Johannisberg Riesling grapes.

MISSION HILL in British Columbia harvests Optima grapes to make its "Late Picked B.A. (Botrytis Affected)" dessert wine.

QUADY in the San Joaquin Valley, California, makes "Elysium" from the Black Muscat grape and "Essensia" from the Orange Muscat grape.

SANTINO in California makes the unusual choice of the Zinfandel grape to produce "Select Late Harvest T.B.A," a botrytized dessert wine.

THURSTON WOLFE in Washington State calls its late-harvest Sauvignon Blanc "Sweet Rebecca."

part two

Fruit

Fruit brandy, or eau de vie, has always been a drink for all seasons. Of ancient lineage, it's made everywhere in the Western world and it utilizes an impressive array of fruits and berries. Once possessed of the art of distillation, the peasant farmer faced with an excess of apples, cherries, pears—any kind of fruit that was sure to rot—knew what to do with it. Distilled, it was preserved until the long winter nights set in. Though the land offered no pear or apple or cherry, there they were, wondrously preserved, at hand, in a bottle.

History has paid scant attention to fruit brandy; political, commercial, and gustatory vicissitudes over centuries drove and still drives the fate of other after-dinner drinks described in this book. Fruit brandies neither graced the Russian royal court nor were embraced by a people made thirsty by war-time embargoes or exorbitant taxes. They did not promise relief from illness nor became a nation's official liquor. They were simple, fiery, and fruity. If they had any purpose beyond the taste in midwinter of a plum or a pear, it was to drill a hole through the early courses of a Rabelesian meal in order to make room for the later courses. At the end of the meal, they were a digestion facilitator. These drinks also go by the name *digestifs.*

Recently, as with grappa, interest in fruit brandies has picked up, and along with it, the quality of the spirits has risen. The fruit brandy distiller aims for the essence of the fruit. With the exceptions of Calvados and one or two others, fruit brandy is aged in glass, not wood. This ensures a pure fruit flavor. And that is the charm of eaux de vie, or what the French also call *alcools blancs* because of their crystalline clearness. The heart of a fruit or berry captured in a glass of clear liquid is no surprise when you consider the immense amounts of produce that go into every bottle of eau de vie. *New York Times* reporter R. W. Apple, in an article on the subject, spoke of a "virtual orchard in your glass."

The principal difference among fruit brandies is, of course, the kind of fruit used. But there are some variations in the manufacturing processes. Seed fruit, or berries, need to be given some assistance through maceration or soaking in a neutral spirit for up to a month because the berries' low sugar content will not produce much alcohol, and heated distillation will affect the berries' delicate flavor. Then the mixture is gently distilled.

Stone fruit is picked at the height of ripeness and mashed with wooden paddles or allowed to collapse into a paste under its own weight. The fruit paste, pits and all, is fermented. Distillation follows in the manner of cognac, the first and last parts, the head and tail, are separated for further processing, and only the center, the heart, is kept for the eau de vie. Generally, fruit brandy is distilled twice in pot stills to a lower proof than that of other spirits in order to retain the most intense fruit flavor. No sugar is ever added. Spring or purified water is added to reduce the alcohol level to the desired proof. The brandy is then transferred to glass or stainless steel containers and aged. A few are aged in wood, the best known being Calvados. There is a French saying to the effect that eaux de vie must be put in the attic. In the old days, the brandy was stored in glass demijohns, stoppered by fabric, under the tile roofs of huge attics. The glass preserved the flavor of the fruit, and the considerable variations in temperature caused evaporation of unpleasant and acrid ingredients.

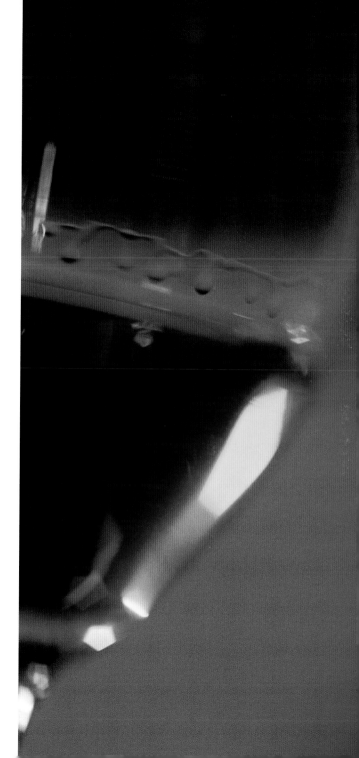

eaux de vie

After apple brandy, which will be discussed separately, the most popular eaux de vie are cherry and plum. My personal favorite is pear. Perhaps seeing pear trees that appeared to be growing bottles biased me. Here is a list of eaux de vie that you should be able to find on a good after-dinner drink list or in a discriminating liquor shop.

Cherry Brandy. (*EAU DE CERISE* in French and *KIRSCH-WASSER* in German.) Some people contend that the finest source of Kirschwasser is the small black wild cherry found in the Rhine Valley. Because of the political geography of the region, this means the fruit can be either French, German, or Swiss. But there is no doubt that it grows in the region that makes the best cherry brandy. The extremely fine

Kirschwasser made by the Zeigler Brothers near Frankfurt, Germany, uses three thousand cherries to make one bottle of brandy. Frequently, a little of the oil from the stones or pits is distilled with the cherry mash to give Kirschwasser a bitter almond taste.

Other producers are Austria's Retter; France's Dettling, Trimbach, and Rene de Miscault; Italy's Jacapo Poli; Switzerland's Etter; and the United States' Bonny Doon and St. George Spirits.

Plum Brandy. (*EAU DE PRUNE* in French.) There are six varieties of plum

used: the yellow mirabelle; the purple quetsch; the violet sloe plum, or prunelle sauvage; the greengage plum, or reine-claude; the prune, or pflumli; and the blue slivovitz, which is aged in wood and hails from Central Europe and the Balkans. While most eaux de vie are clear, some of the plum brandies can take on a yellow or green tint. They use lots of fruit: ten pounds of mirabelles go into each bottle of the eponymously named brandy.

Some brand names to look for are France's René de Miscault Vieille Prune and Quetsch; Trimbach Prunelle Sauvage and Mirabelle; and Massenez for a variety of plum brandies, including mirabelle, wild sloe, and blue plum; Italy's Capovilla Prugne; and Switzerland's Etter Pflumli Prune.

Pear Brandy. (*EAU DE POIRE* in French.) The Williams pear, the

familiar Bartlett, is the pear of choice in pear brandy, or poire Williams. About thirty pounds of the fruit go into each bottle. The pear and the apple seem to me to be the fruits that most beautifully give themselves over to the distiller's art. The best poire Williams really do imprison the essence of the fruit; that is what you smell and taste in the glass, not the alcohol, and that is as it should be. It is difficult enough, even in the finest farmers' markets, to find and handle a pear at its zenith of ripeness; one can imagine the challenge facing the brandy maker. A charming although not altogether useful distinction of pear brandy–making is the occasional practice of growing a whole pear inside the bottle intended to receive the brandy. Romantically,

The Brave New World of Eaux de Vie

For centuries, the production and consumption of eaux de vie has been a local endeavor, confined for the most part to France's Alsace and the Rhône Valley, the Black Forest and the Rhine Valley areas of Germany, and the German-speaking areas of Switzerland. Things are changing. Alsace's G. E. Massenez, a principal fruit brandy maker, has its own Web site and ships around the world.

Alsatians Gilbert Miclo and Jean-Paul Metté not only make fine mainstream fruit brandy but engage in interesting experiments. Miclo's operation includes à range of brandies made from tropical fruits such as coconut, mango, and pineapple. Metté has distilled truffles, mint leaves, and cumin. His current fascination is a *eau de bale de houx* (the holly berry) and an *eau de prunelle sauvage* (made from wild plums called sloes, which used to share the spotlight with the juniper berry in Sloe Gin Fizzes). Massenez also makes cutting edge eaux de vie, including one from holly berries, which it describes as reminiscent of underbrush with hints of moss and mushrooms, and recommends accompanying it with smoked salmon.

The newcomers to the world of *alcools blancs* are American. Two have very different philosophies. St. George Spirits is located in the San Francisco Bay Area. Founded by Alsatian Jorge Rupf, the eau de vie maker claims to combine hand-crafted European distilling equipment with modern California wine-making techniques. He searches for fruit throughout the Northwest — pears from Lake County, California; raspberries from Oregon; and cherries from Washington. By not having to grow the fruit himself, he protects himself from agricultural vagaries; he can choose the best fruit, wherever it is raised.

Another American brandy maker is Clear Creek, near Portland, Oregon, whose pear orchard owner, Steve McCarthy, calculates that selling the fruit directly costs more than raising and picking it. He devoted a great deal of time to learning the art of fruit brandy distillation in Europe. At least one expert taster rates Clear Creek's pear brandy as his all-time favorite eau de vie.

Yet another American is Randall Graham, owner of Bonny Doon, in Santa Cruz, California. In addition to grappa, he makes excellent fruit brandies, among them, pear, cherry, plum, apricot, and nectarine.

this incarcerated pear is called the *prisonnier.* I have always suspected it takes up space better filled by the real thing.

Austria's Retter makes fine poire, as do France's Massenez, Rene de Miscault, and Trimbach. Italy's Jacopo Poli and Switzerland's Etter, my favorite, make top-flight poire. The United States' Clear Creek and St. George Spirits make first-rate pear brandy.

Raspberry Brandy. (*EAU DE FRAMBOISE* in French.) Because of their

low sugar content, seed fruit or berries are macerated in brandy for about a month, in a ratio of 100 kilos of berries to 25 liters of 100-proof eau de vie. Slight fermentation takes place during this time, and then the mixture is distilled. Massenez claims to have perfected the making of this berry eau de vie in 1913. *Eau de framboise* is one of the most popular fruit brandies. It is, true to its source, perhaps the most elegant of fruit brandies. (The wild strawberry, *fraise de bois,* is also made into a brandy, but not in the volume of *framboise.*) One of the most delightful apéritifs offered in France is the champagne *framboise:* it is like a Kir Royale, but instead of cassis, a tablespoon or two of raspberry brandy flavors the champagne. Some makers go as far away as Romania for their fruit. Eighteen pounds of wild raspberries go into one bottle of the brandy.

Some *framboise* makers to look for are producers of other eaux de vie: Austria's Retter; France's Massenez, Etienne Brana, Rene de Miscault, and Trimbach; Italy's Jacopo Poli; Switzerland's Etter; and the United States' St. George Spirits.

Peach Brandy. (*EAU DE PÊCHE* in French.) I have not seen this eau de

vie in the United States, although I did have a wonderful one in Provence—Arles, to be specific. It's worth seeking out. Massenez makes peach as one of their wide range of eaux de vie.

The Infinite (Almost) Variety of
Eaux de Vie

Here is an array of materials that have gone into eaux de vie. Not all are fruits. If you visit Alsace, you can buy a sampler pack of miniatures that will provide a tour of a handful of these resourceful spirits.

Apricot (HUNGARIAN: *Barack palinka*)

Blackberry

Black Currant (FRENCH: *Cassis*)

Blood orange

Blueberry

Celery (FRENCH: *Celeri*)

Cherry (FRENCH: *Cerise*; GERMAN: *Kirsch*)

Coconut

Cumin

Elderberry

Gentian

Ginger

Holly berry (FRENCH: *Baie de houx*)

Huckleberry (FRENCH: *Myrtille*)

Mango

Mulberry

Peach (FRENCH: *Pêche*)

Pear (FRENCH: *Poire*)

Pine buds (FRENCH: *Sapin*)

Pineapple

Plum

Quince (FRENCH: *Coing*)

Raspberry (FRENCH: *Framboise*)

Rose hips (FRENCH: *Gratte-cul*)

Rowanberry (FRENCH: *Sorbe*)

Strawberry (FRENCH: *Fraise*)

Truffles

Wild Mint

Wild Strawberry (FRENCH: *Fraise de bois*)

There are different opinions about how to approach a fine eau de vie. Most agree the glass should be frosted, and I prefer the spirit to be chilled. A member of the Massenez family recommends keeping eaux de vie made from stone fruits in the refrigerator and those made from seed fruits in the freezer. A good recommendation, I say. Many restaurants keep their eaux de vie chilled. Failing that, I've had the bar run the drink through a martini shaker filled with ice. As with cognac and other fine grape brandies, balloon-shaped glasses are frowned upon, and narrow bowled glasses, such as the sherry *copita,* are smiled upon. Especially with eaux de vie, you want the aroma to funnel undiminished right into your olfactory system. In Verona, Italy, I drank poire Williams from an elegant chilled glass shaped like a tube six inches high, and no more than an inch in diameter, the aroma emerging from a slightly larger but squatter cylinder that held the measure of pear quintessence.

CALVADOS

Apple brandy is simply hard cider distilled. But there are apple brandies and there are apple brandies. The American apple brandy is called applejack. The basic French apple brandy is called *eau-de-vie de-cidre de Normandie,* or *de Bretagne,* or *du Maine,* designating where it was made. And then there is Calvados. Calvados is a *département* in Normandy, the heart of France's cider and apple brandy country. The apple brandy from Calvados is unique, and so usually considered apart from other fruit brandies. When given the premier designation of *Calvados du Pays d'Auge,* it not only has all the attributes of the best eaux de vie—the essence of the fruit—but the finesse of a fine cognac. It is different from, and much superior to, the other distilled hard ciders.

The Vikings were said to enjoy Calvados on their raids into Normandy. For centuries, the Normans have used Calvados as an

Bottle
at
40%
Alc/V

Product of Franc

aid to digestion, not only at the end of the meal, but in the middle. When this operation is required, the brandy makes what is called the *le trou norman,* the Norman hole, to make room for more hearty Norman cuisine.

Eight hundred different kinds of apples are grown in Normandy. They fall into five basic groups: bitter (rich in tannin), sweet (for alcohol content), acid (for tang), sour and bittersweet (to act as stabilizers). Each maker of Calvados selects a combination of apples each October and November. After the fruit is pressed, the juice is separated from the mash and ferments for about six weeks, until it reaches an alcohol level of at least 4.5 percent. The spirit is doubly distilled in pot stills, like cognac. At around 140 proof, it is ready for aging. One bottle of Calvados will require about sixty pounds of apples or twenty liters of the fermented cider.

The aging process makes Calvados unique among eaux de vie. Fine-grained oak from the Limousin or Tronçais forests is the choice for barrels, and the interactions of the wood, air, and spirit give the brandy, as it does with cognac, complexity of flavor and its characteristic amber color. The cellar master plays a large role in determining the nature of Calvados. Most Calvados are aged for less than ten years, but some are left in oak for as long as four or five decades, becoming quite remarkable. When bottled, Calvados is between 80 and 84 proof.

In tasting, look for the apple first in any Calvados. The aging brings smoothness, even silkiness, and flavors of vanilla, almonds, walnuts, citrus, and, of course, oak and tannin.

Chateau du Breuil makes a Bizouard "hors d'âge," a blend of Calvados that is at least fifteen years old. Other fine Calvados to look for are Daron's XO Pays d'Auge and 1955 Pays d'Auge and Herout Hors d'Age Médaille d'Or. The better Calvados are not cheap. But think of it this way. One bottle of the amber elixir will provide you with an apple a day for several months.

part three # Grain

The Scots and Canadians spell it whisky; the

Americans and Irish spell it whiskey. The ancient Gaels spelled it *uisquebaugh.* Pronounce it with a wheeze and a gargle and you have *whis-ga-baw,* which easily becomes whiskey. It means aqua vitae, eau de vie, or, in plain English, "water of life."

Early in the Dark Ages, Christian monks returning to Ireland after proselytizing abroad brought back the Middle Eastern secret of distillation, of making whiskey. Outside the calm and learning of the monastery walls, the Dark Ages were a time of poverty, misery, ignorance, war, pillaging, and plague. The monks sought edibles and potables that had medicinal and restorative virtues and they were pleased to find primordial whiskey. By the twelfth century, Irish and whiskey were inseparable.

The spirit and its method of distillation crossed over to the rugged, dank coast of Scotland, where it was warmly embraced by a hardy people whose stone huts were heated only by peat. In Scotland and in Ireland the making of whiskey from malted barley or wheat was elevated into an art form.

Residents of the New World did not begin consuming whiskey until considerably later. Rum and Madeira were of economic necessity the most popular early American drinks. Not until the 1700s, following the immigration of thousands of Irish, Scots, and Germans, did an interest in distilling grain take hold. When it did, corn would be the cereal of opportunity.

All whiskeys are made the same fundamental way. They require grain, water, and yeast. The grain is cooked, mashed, fermented (whiskey is basically distilled beer without the hops), distilled, and matured in wood casks. But there are remarkable differences in the finished product; the variables include the type of still, the number of distillations, the strains of yeast, the nature of wood and the "toastedness" of the barrel, the number of years aged, the water source, and, of course, the kind of cereal used— corn, barley, wheat, rye, or oats.

Throughout their considerable history whiskeys have supplied much all-purpose booze, most of it barely palatable. The drink killed pain and fomented riots, increased conviviality and drove people to poverty. As part of the social rather than the political side of recent American life, whiskey, often rye, has been utilized as a preprandial, taken with water or soda, or as a base for a cocktail, requiring a mixer.

Whiskey was the inspiration for much slang, most of it pejorative, from the nineteenth-century's "moonshine" and "bootlegger" to Prohibition's "speakeasy" and "teetotaler." Whiskey probably has no more romantic association than in the Hollywood Western: a solitary cowboy enters a bar through swinging doors, passes by all manner of sin and outrage erupting at tables around him; weary from the saddle and a world of hurt; he plants a boot on the brass rail and orders whiskey; a corked bottle and a shot glass are set before him. Solace is his.

Nowadays, when we plant a Gucci-shod foot on the brass rail, we order by brand name. Today, the style is to seek quality rather than solace, taste rather than price. And three kinds of whiskey have found their way onto after-dinner drink lists, a recent phenomenon. They are the ones that interest us in this book. First, bourbon, in three premium subsets, single barrel, small batch, and pot still. Then Tennessee whiskey, which is a kind of bourbon, but with an important difference. Last but not least, single malt Scotch, thought by its devotees to be equal to, if not better than, the finest cognac or the rarest port. All these fine finishes to a superb meal are served and drunk neat, and savored for the care and flavor that their makers put into them.

bourbon

Bourbon is a purely American liquor and the pride of Kentucky. It is derived from corn, but other grains are involved. Bourbon must be at least 51 percent corn; at more than 80 percent, by federal law it is denominated corn whiskey.

We still think of bourbon in the genteel context of lush grass, horses, antebellum mansions, and branch water. The basis of the mint julep. On the other hand, we think of corn whiskey as the product made by the light of the moon by that quintessential American folk character, the hillbilly. This drink was celebrated in the cartoon strip L'il Abner as "Kickapoo Joy Juice." A more modern, urban image of bourbon has a hard-bitten edge to it; it is the hard-boiled private eye's preferred eye-opener and the preprandial of choice in yesterday's steak-and-chop houses pungent with the smoke of burning cigarettes and beef fat.

Bourbon is still the foundation of a perfect Manhattan, and mint juleps are delightful before viewing the Kentucky Derby on TV, and no doubt there are still those who enjoy a bourbon and ginger ale—a "highball." But recently, connoisseurs of American whiskey have developed a regard for the most carefully crafted of this spirit, and especially after a good meal. It has a flavor all its own, as the smoky peat flavor defines Scotch, a combination of complex tastes produced by the sour-mash, the charred barrel, the Kentucky air, a taste of cereal, fruit, and spice.

The first American whiskey was made in Staten Island, New York, in 1640. There wasn't much of a market for whiskey, however. Rum, cheaply made and plentiful because of the vigorous trade between the colonies and the Caribbean, was the liquor of choice. The coastal climate in the colonies was not conducive to the growing of grain, so the whiskey could hardly compete with rum made from sugarcane molasses.

Matters changed in the 1700s. The mother country, England, imposed a tax on all sugar, molasses, and rum imported from "any of the colonies or possessions of or under the dominion of His Majesty." The tax was aimed to eliminate the main competition, the merchants of the French West Indies. But it stimulated another competitor, the American farmer-distiller.

In the mid-1700s, many colonists, the first pioneers, began moving westward, into the wildlands of Virginia, Pennsylvania, and the Carolinas. At the same time, immigrant Irish, Scots, and Germans, each from a country with a long distilling tradition, poured into the colonies. The western lands were agreeable to the cultivation of grain, mostly rye, which imported from Europe, grew quickly and hardily. Distillation followed quite naturally. Liquor keeps for quite a long time and is easy to transport—one horse could carry either four bushels of grain or a sixty-gallon barrel of whiskey. Twenty-four bushels of grain went into that barrel. So with excess grain about to spoil and a lively market in neighboring communities, the economics of whiskey production were irresistible to the farmer-distiller.

By the Revolution, the making of whiskey had become an industry. George Washington produced rye whiskey at Mount Vernon and sold it profitably. Indeed, during the Revolutionary War he worried that his troops, unable

Bottled in Bond

Many whiskey drinkers think that a bourbon carrying the declaration Bottled in Bond is an assurance of quality. It is and it isn't. The history of whiskey making involves battles between distillers and Uncle Sam's tax collectors and revenuers. Many times taxes on the spirit have threatened the industry. For example, draconian taxes levied on new whiskey, which had years to age, crippled the industry during the Civil War. The riposte to these taxes was a dramatic increase in the availability of "white lightning" or "white dog." Eventually, tax authorities created a tax stamp to be affixed to all spirits made in America. The distiller was granted a grace period to pay, provided the liquor be kept in supervised "bonded" warehouses.

Several variations on this scheme were enacted in the late nineteenth century. In 1897, the Bottled in Bond Act added some provisions that did indeed insure certain qualities to the bonded whiskey. It provided temporary relief from the excise tax if the whiskey were at least four years old, distilled at one plant by one proprietor, and bottled at 100 proof, under the supervision of the Treasury Department. And the whiskey had to be straight, no blends, please. A few more changes in the law occurred during the twentieth century. The law guarantees that makers meet certain quantitative standards, including labeling, and they do not have to pay the tax until the booze is shipped.

to pay the extortionist prices of the farmer-distillers, went wanting for whiskey: he proposed "erecting Public Distilleries in different states."

After the war, President Washington, needing capital for the start-up of the new nation, levied an excise tax on liquor. The ensuing Whiskey Rebellion drove many unhappy farmers to the new state of Kentucky to escape the tax collectors. They grew corn and combined it with the pure, iron-free water that bubbled up from springs through the limestone mantle of the region to make a distinctive new whiskey.

This bourbon whiskey most likely got its name because it was shipped from the Kentucky river port of Limestone, in Bourbon County. Bourbon was on its way to a turbulent history, marked by booms, conflicts with tax collectors and the consequent business of moonshining, the practice of bootlegging (during the Civil War, illicit whiskey was smuggled to troops in the tops of boots), and a whiskey scandal during Ulysses S. Grant's presidency. Distillers faced economic busts when legislation during World War I made distillation illegal, and in 1920, when Prohibition was enacted. Whiskey was rationed during World War II. It wasn't until the 1950s, 1960s, and 1970s that bourbon warmed the throats and hearts of Americans in any degree comparable to its demand in the nineteenth century. In 1964, an Act of Congress officially designated bourbon as the national spirit.

Most bourbons consist of 60 to 75 percent corn, although only 51 percent is required to give it the name bourbon. Rye or wheat, but not both, is also used, and a lesser portion of malted barley. These other grains contribute characteristic flavors and aromas to the spirit.

Each distiller has its own strain of yeast, which gives that maker's bourbon a distinctive taste. The yeasting process used to make bourbon is called sour-mash. This means that 25 percent of the fermenting liquor must be "stillage" or "backset," the residue of mash from the previous distillation.

Bourbon is distilled twice. First, the liquid goes into a continuous or beer still to become a "low wine." Then this stage of the whiskey is distilled again, into a "high wine." This is now new bourbon, which by law can be no more than 160 proof. Then water is used to cut the whiskey to between 105 and 110 proof. The water is naturally sweet, free of iron and rich in calcium and

The nature of the barrel and aging process is especially important. All bourbon must be aged in new, charred, white oak for at least two years. White oak from cold forests, such as those in northern Minnesota, is preferred. The wood grain is denser because the trees grow more slowly in the harsher climate. The wood is dried in a temperature controlled warehouse for thirty days. It is said that Maker's Mark, a premium bourbon, incurs the higher cost of leaving the wood in the open air for up to three years because this reduces the bitterness in the wood. After the drying, the wood is heated to reduce the moisture in it. The barrels are then assembled. They will have a fifty-three-gallon capacity, and when full of bourbon, weigh about five hundred pounds.

After the barrels are constructed, they are charred or "toasted" over a controlled but intense fire for one or two minutes. There are four levels of char, from light char to deep char. The deeper the char, the deeper the color, aroma, and flavor of the bourbon. During the charring process, the starches in the wood are converted into sugars. By char level three, the sap is caramelized by the heat, creating a vanilla-like flavor and forming the "red layer" that will contribute to the character of a premium bourbon. After being filled with bourbon, the barrels are stored in warehouses on racks or ricks designed to allow air to flow around the barrels.

magnesium, both considered good for whiskey making.

After-dinner bourbons are usually one of three types of ultra-premium whiskeys: single-barrel, small-batch, and pot-still bourbon. Single-barrel bourbons come from only one barrel, and the details of its manufacture are often handwritten on the bottle's label. These bourbons have received special treatment by being singled out by the master distiller as exemplary of a particular style.

Small-batch bourbons were introduced in the 1980s. They are not necessarily distilled in small batches. The maker of Jim Beam offered this definition: "small-batch bourbons are rare and exceptional bourbons married from select barrels from a cross section of barrels in the rackhouse. This ensures quality and consistency of flavor and character. Each small-batch bourbon has a unique aroma and taste which is credited to its unique recipe, aging, and proof. We do not rotate because the small-batch process is based on marrying barrels from select levels where they pick up distinct characteristics depending on location in the rackhouse."

The Best of the Best

Fine single-barrel bourbons to look for are Blanton's, Rock Hill Farms, Elmer T. Lee, Benchmark, Hancock's Reserve, and Wild Turkey's Kentucky Spirit. If it's a small-batch bourbon you want, try Jim Beam (Booker's), Knob Creek, Baker's, Basil Hayden, and Woodford Reserve.

However, if you want to seek out the best of the best, here are an expert's recommendations. For a pot still: A. H. Hirsch's "20-Year-Old Pot Still Straight Bourbon" (made, interestingly, in Pennsylvania). F. Paul Pacult gives it his highest recommendation, and finds flavors of mint, banana, brown sugar, maple, and red fruit, to name several. For small-batch, he gives his highest recommendation to Baker's "7-Year-Old Kentucky Straight Bourbon/Small-Batch," noting that Baker's is the most cognac-like American whiskey out there. Single-barrel: he highly recommends Blanton's "Single-Barrel Kentucky Straight Bourbon; Barrel No. 444, Rick No. 9, Warehouse H — Bottled in Oct. 1993." He gives the highest marks to Maker's Mark "Limited-Edition Kentucky Straight Bourbon," calling it "truly one of the great whiskeys available anywhere at any price."

Tennessee. whiskey

One other special bourbon deserves note. The expensive, slow, work-intensive pot still of yesteryear has mostly been replaced by the continuous still. But a few bourbon makers still create limited editions using the old-fashioned copper pot, with its long, graceful, swanlike neck uncurling from its rotund, onion-shaped chamber. Pot-still bourbon is considered to be more flavorful than that produced in any other way.

Tennessee is almost as famous as Kentucky for its whiskey, but it has only two distilleries, Jack Daniels and George Dickel. What the state lacks in breadth of product line, it makes up for in volume and brand recognition. Jack Daniels is a global best-seller, found on the top shelves of bars in Paris, Tokyo, London, and Rome, as well as Nashville and Manhattan. "J. D." or "Mister Jack" is a request a drinker can utter with confidence.

Tennessee does not want its whiskey known as bourbon; it wants the liquor to be called "Tennessee sour mash." First, it wants to retain pride of place. Second, the making of the whiskey departs from bourbon in one important regard. Because this whiskey derives flavors from outside the cask-aging process, it cannot legally call itself bourbon. It has the corn, the yeast, and the aging in wood. However, it adds a step before placing the new spirit in oak barrels. Tennessee whiskey is filtered through ten-foot-high vats of sugar-maple charcoal, a system known as the Lincoln County Process. The process takes seven to ten days and mellows out the whiskey. It removes some unwanted flavors, refines the liquor, and adds flavors of its own. It results in a more full-bodied drink than bourbon. Its predominant flavor has been described as "sooty-sweet."

"From the bonny bells of heather
They brewed a drink long-syne,

Was sweeter far than honey.
Was stronger far than wine."

—ROBERT LOUIS STEVENSON

SINGLE MALT SCOTCH

From the sixth century to the mid–nineteenth century, Scotch whisky was largely unknown outside of Scotland and England. There was no whisky industry as such, and each laird probably had a still that supplied neighbors and a little outside trade. No doubt, the Scotch of those years was harsh and smoky, imbued with the taste of peat (a kind of pre-coal consisting of partially carbonized vegetable matter, largely heather, formed in bogs).

In 1853, Andrew Usher began to blend Scotch whisky for sale. Britannia then ruled the world, or at least much of it, and the demand for a taste of home far exceeded any supply the malt distilleries could provide. He mixed malt spirit with grain whisky and produced a lighter, less expensive, more consistent, and significantly larger supply of whisky. Usher also used a vastly more efficient continuous or patent still instead of the old-fashioned pot still. Blended Scotch whisky *was*

Scotch whisky until the 1980s when, inexplicably, blended Scotch whisky sales began to decline and the market for single malt Scotch shot skyward. It is malt Scotch, made only in Scotland only from malted barley, in a pot still, cask-aged for at least three years, that we find on after-dinner drink menus. Now, single malt Scotch is the choice of the connoisseur. Alas, the lairds of history are not around to savor the irony.

Malt Scotch is made similarly to bourbon, in five stages. The first is malting, whereby the barley partially germinates and is known as green malt. It is then dried and cooked, usually over a peat fire. The second stage is mashing. Whether using corn for bourbon or malted barley for Scotch, cooking the grain converts starches into sugars, without which the grain would not ferment. The cooked grain is steeped in warm water and mixed. Fermentation is the third step. In a separate vat, the yeast initiates the transformation of the sugars into alcohol. What we now have is beer, without the hops. The Scots and Irish call it "wash." The fourth stage is distillation. The fermented liquid is boiled in pot stills. As the vapors rise, they are condensed in coolers, two or three times, becoming whisky. As with cognac and bourbon, the first and last parts of the distillation ("foreshots" and "feints") are separated from the middle, the cognac-maker's "heart," and redistilled to eliminate impurities. The last step is the maturation of the whisky in oak, by law for at least three years. Here the individual Scotch will develop much of its characteristic flavors and its amber color. Different kinds of barrels, often previously used to age bourbon and sherry, and the water used to reduce the proof, contribute to the individuality of the final product.

Perhaps as much as the great wines of France and cognac, the distinctive qualities of single malt Scotches are determined by place. Scotches differ dramatically by region, and even within a region variations abound. Islay, a treeless island that is part of the Inner Hebrides, off the central western coast of Scotland, is home to eight distilleries. One writer on Scotch, Daniel Lerner, observes that two of them, "a stone's throw from each other, produce whiskies that smell and taste as different from each other as vanilla and licorice do." This phenomenon gives single malt devotees great pleasure, because, despite the spirit's relative scarcity (5 percent or less of all Scotch whisky production) and its restricted geography (four regions, including a few islands, of a smallish country), it presents the drinker with a wide variety of characteristics to experience and enjoy.

There are four regions of whisky production in Scotland.

The Lowlands.

This region is located in the south, just below Glasgow and Edinburgh. Although most Lowlands whisky goes into blends, the single malts are light, delicate, fruity, and lack the smoke of peat and smack of sea that characterize their cousins to the north.

Campbeltown.

This region is located on a peninsula on the west coast. Only two operating distilleries remain, but one, Springbank, is thought to be among Scotland's best. The sea exerts a strong influence on Campbeltown's Scotch.

Islay.

This island just north of Campbeltown commands a view of Northern Ireland. Eight distilleries make single malts here that are known for their heft and pungency, their strong flavors of peat, smoke, seaweed, and brine. One writer commented that some, such as Laphroaig and Ardberg, can be "bullies."

The Highlands.

This largest district is home to the majority of distilleries. It includes cities such as Aberdeen and Perth and stretches north to the Orkney Islands, as well as to the northeast and northwest coasts and islands (not to mention Loch Ness). The landscape is mostly spare, the climate severe. (As a single malt producer, it deserves to be segmented more precisely, and several writers do just that.) The malts produced here are mesomorphs, full of the flavors of peat, and on the coasts, the sea.

Part of the Highlands, Speyside, extending inland from the northeast coast, is usually described separately. It is thought to be the finest area in Scotland—and thus the world—for creating whisky. A web of rivers, including the Spey, Avon, Findhorn, Fiddich, and Livet, carrying pure waters from springs and lochs, crisscross the region. Unlike the rest of the Highlands, Speyside is lush. Home to over forty distilleries, it produces whisky in a wide range of styles. Mellow,

SCALE OF MILES

0 5 10   20   30   40   50   60

ORKNEY ISLANDS
Stromness   Hoy   S. Ronaldsha

Valley   Noss I.
Sheila Ness   ZZLERWICK
Burra Is.   Bressa I.
Foula I.   Sandwick   Sumburgh Hd
Long. W. 2 from Green.

Pentland Firth
Cape Wrath
Dunnet Hd   Dunnet   Duncansby Hd
Swarthy Hd   Duncansby
Sandwood B.   Dunness   Thurso   John O'Groats
Butt of Lewis
L. Laxford   Durness   Farr   Dale   Bruen   Noss Hd
Tolstay   Tongue   WICK
Barvas   Edderachillis   Rainsdale   More   Latheron
Stornaway   L. Assynt   L. Naver   B. Klibreck   CAITHNESS
L. Bernera   Assynt   Bramore
The Aird   Loch Shin   Balnafrech   Kildonan
Dundiat   Shi ness   Brora
Stornaway Hd   SUTHERLAND
Gallan Hd   Lochs   L. Inard   Lairg   Golspie
Uig   L'Athliner   Shell   Ben More Hills   DORNOCH
Sampl   Taransay   Dornock Firth
Pibb.g   Tarbet   Malvee   Flowerdale   Ben Deoig   Tarbat Ness
Harris   Harris Sound   PART of CROMARTY
North Uist   Garloch   Kincardine   TAIN
Aird Pt   Garloch   Ben Laris   Ben Wyvis   Murray Firth
Uig   Erri dale   CROMARTY   Burgh
THE MINCH   L. Torridon   Fort rose   ELGIN   BANFF
Benbecula   Torridon   Beauley   Fochabers   Turriff   Fraser...
South Uist   Applecross   Dingwall   Rothes   Keith   Peterhead
Lockcarron   Beauley R.   Dufftown   Huntly   Newburgh
Scalad   Ardnaff   INVERNESS   Shanwell   Inverury   Meldr.
Barra   Mealfour vouny   Dores   Grantown   Leemore
Vatersay   Strath   Cantray   BANFF
Ben Attow   Tomantoul   Alford   Kincardine   ABERDEEN
Barra Hd   Ballen datch   Cairngorm   Ben Muchui   Deebank
Cana   L. Eishan   Ft of Foyers   SM   Balaster   Craithie
Rum I.   INVERNESS   Ft Augustus   Kinginsie   Braemar   STONE
Eig I.   Nevis   Loch bucky   Laggan   HAVEN
Much I.   L. Shiel   L. Laggan   Greenburgh   KINCARDIN
CoII I.   L. Eil   Spean R.   CRAMPIAN   Fordoun
Balehough   Ardnamurchan   Ft William   Treagh   Blair Athol   Clava   Lawrencekirk   Bervie
Tirree I.   Ben Nevis   R. Tay   Killiecrankie   Kilburn   Brechin
Hynish   Tobermory   R. Tummel   Kirriemuir   FORFAR   Montrose
Ulva I.   MULL   Appin   Lydoch   Aberfeldy   Blairgowrie   Glammis   Arbroath
Staffa   Ben More   L. Rannoch   L. Etive   Ben Lawers   Dunkeld   Cupar Angus   Dundee
Icolmkill I.   Bunaw   Kalpin   Kenmore   Scone H   Firth of Tay
long.   Oban   B. Cruachan   L. Earn   Crieff   PERTH   St Andrews
Seil I.   Kilmore   Ben More   Muthill   Aberneth   Fife Ness
ARGYLE   L. Awe   Vorlich   Callander   Newburgh   Crail
P. Prua   INVERARY   L. Katrine   B. Ledi   CUPAR   Anstruther
Scarba I.   B. Lomond   Doune   Kinross   Leven   Dysart
Colonsay I.   Melfort   L. Lomond   KINROSS   Firth of Forth
Oronsay I.   Lochgilhead   STIRLING   CLACKMAN   Kirkcaldy
Tarbert   Kilmun   Helensburgh   Dunferm line   N. Berwick
Askaig   Kilmorie   DUMBARTON   Falkirk   Leith   Dunbar
ISLAY   Jura   Greenock   LINLITHGOW   HADDINGTON
Bowmore   RENFREW   GLASGOW   Calder   EDINBURGH   HADDINGTON
Kintra   ROTHSAY   Paisley   Hamilton   Dalkeith   Eve...
Mull of Islay   Largs   Carluke   Linton   Lauder   BERWICK
Drumore   Dunlop   LANARK   PEEBLES   Greenlaw
Saddle   Brodick   Irvine   Biggar   Kelso
Malin Hd   Kilbride   Kilmarnock   Douglas   PEEBLES   Yarrow   Melrose
Rathlin I.   ARRAN   Catrine   Muirkirk   SELKIRK   JEDBURG
CANTIRE   R. Ayr   Sanquhar   Ettrick   Hawick   ROXBURGH
Campbeltown   AYR   Mayhole   Thornhill   Moffat   Carter fell
Mull of Cantire   Girvan   L. Doon   New Castleton   Cheviot Hills
Coleraine   Ballantrae   Minnhive   Langholm
Loch Ryan   Craiglee   New   DUMFRIES   Longtown
Londonderry   Kirkcoln   Galloway   Milton   Annan   Gretna Green
Stranraer   KIRKCUDBRIGHT   Castle Douglas   Carlisle
WIGTON   Creetown

IRELAND

ATLANTIC OCEAN   NORTH SEA   NORTH CHANNEL   HEBRIDES or WESTERN ISLES   LITTLE MINCH   ISLE OF SKYE

delicate, elegant, and subtle are words that have been used to describe Speyside malts. Glenlivet and Macallan are two of the better-known distilleries of the region.

The islands of the Highlands include Mull, Skye, and Jura in the west, which are part of the Inner Hebrides, and the Orkneys in the northeast. Malts from the islands tend to be strong and smoky.

Obvious differences related to peatiness or brininess are imparted to single malt Scotch by virtue of geography. But geography alone does not account for the enormous variety and range of individuality in a spirit that begins simply enough, with barley, yeast, and water. The *terroir,* the influence of the environment and craft, takes on new meaning with single malts. Here are some of the influential factors.

The water used in making single malt is pure and untreated. If it flows over peat, it will give the whisky that flavor. If it flows over granite, a softer whisky will result. One scholar, Dr. P. Schidrowitz, has asserted that the best water is that which has its origin as a spring that has risen through red granite and then runs through peaty land or a heather-filled moor on its way to the distillery.

The malting process also plays a role in flavor. Traditionally, distilleries use a peat fire to dry-kiln barley. Some use higher percentages of peat than others. Some do not use peat at all. The flavor of the whisky will be affected by the distiller's choice. ("Peat reek" is a term used to describe whiskies, such as Laphroaig, that favor the heavy use of peat.)

The structure and condition of the still is also important. Taller stills produce a lighter, clearer spirit, because the vapors travel farther to reach the condenser; shorter, squatter stills produce lustier whisky. Glenmorangie is an example of the former, said to be made in the tallest still in the Highlands, and Macallan an example of the latter. Distillers needing to replace a still have been known to have every dent, crease, and dimple replicated in the new one in an effort to ensure the perpetuation of their particular style of whisky.

The cask affects the Scotch as well. Single malt must be aged for at least three years. Most spend much more time in wood, some over twenty years. Oak is the wood of choice; it is plentiful, and porous, which provides the oxygen the whisky needs to mature. Different kinds of barrels are employed to impart specific tastes to the whisky. Charred oak barrels that have been used to age bourbon are popular, as are barrels that have held sherry. Bourbon barrels give the whisky a caramelized taste reminiscent of vanilla. Sherry barrels impart sweet winy tastes. Some makers are experimenting with barrels that have first aged port, brandy, or rum. In some cases, a whisky will spend years in a bourbon or sherry cask, and then be finished in another barrel that readied a different spirit for the bottle.

And, last but not least, as with cognac, the location of the warehouse is a significant influence on the whisky. The salt air will permeate the whisky barrels in seaside warehouses. Wherever located, the aging whisky contracts in the winter, and the porous barrels breathe in the local atmosphere.

All of these influences, some controlled, some intended, and some submitted to, interact to produce a unique whisky. The most skilled still master is said to be able to detect 150 different fragrances in a sample of whiskey.

Just as oenophiles have their tastings, why not do the same with Scotch? A tasting can be formal or informal, but it should promote conviviality, educate the nose and palate, and even be good for an argument or two. One way to do it is to select, say, six single malts from different regions and in different styles. Prepare a single page form on which tasters can judge different qualities and flavors. Leave room at the bottom for a handwritten comment. The vocabulary of wine-tasting applies to Scotch: tasters can evaluate color, nose (smell), mouth (taste), body (weight), fullness (strength), depth (complexity), and finish (aftertaste). Offer a checklist of adjectives that further characterize aroma and flavor of the single malt: smoky, peaty, silky, smooth, fruity, spicy, salty, oily. The idea of a tasting is to get to know the individuality of whisky, not to rate one against the other. The whisky should be tasted neat, at room temperature. There are varying thoughts about the kind of glass that should be used. A brandy snifter is recommended, but a tumbler or conventional wine glass will do. Look, smell, and taste. Don't swirl, and don't spit.

Here are some suggestions for whiskies to select from and their provenance. Each comes in a number of ages. Bladnoch (Lowlands), Bowmore (Islay), Clynelish (northern Highlands), Cragannmore (Speyside), Dalwhinnie (central Highlands), Deanston (southern Highlands), Glen Garioch (eastern Highlands), Glen Scotia (Campbeltown), Glenfarcas (Speyside), Glenlivet (Speyside), Glenmorangie (northern Highlands), Highland Park (Orkney Island), Isle of Jura (Jura Island), Longmorn (Speyside), The Macallan (Speyside), Oban (western Highlands), Springbank (Campbeltown), Talisker (Skye Island), and Tobermory (Mull Island). This small sampling offers a broad range of styles and regions.

The traditional Scots' toast is pronounced SHLAN-jer. *Slainte!*

part four Exotica

A few after-dinner drinks no longer in vogue deserve a mention. These exotica, or plant liqueurs, do not fit the three main food groups of grape, fruit, and grain, but instead utilize just about everything from the rest of the plant kingdom: barks, roots, spices, herbs, flowers, seeds, beans, fruits, and nuts. These ingredients are added to an alcohol base, usually brandy, and distilled.

While politics has played a major role in the development of such after-dinner libations as port and cognac, religion has been the influence on plant liqueurs, which the Christian monks developed in the Middle Ages. The drinks were created not as a soothing finish to a good meal but as medicines, restoratives, and digestive aids in a time when ills were many and medical skills few. If the elixir of herbs failed to cure a malady, the alcohol undoubtably made it easier to bear.

These liqueurs are served at room temperature, and in small doses.

bénédictine
and B&B

The oldest liqueur in the Western world is D.O.M. Bénédictine, created in the Bénédictine Abbey of Fécamp, France, in 1510 as an antidote to malaria. The abbreviation, D.O.M., which appears on every label, stands for *Dio Optimo Maximo,* "To God, most good, most great." After a hard day of prayer, a sip or two of this liqueur was no doubt relaxing.

The formula for Bénédictine is one of the world's best-kept secrets. The production moved from the religious order to a private corporation in 1863, but the secret has been kept. It is said only three persons know the complete recipe. At the distillery, there is a *Salon de Contrefaçons,* the "Hall of Counterfeits," which displays hundreds of attempted imitations.

The liqueur is made from twenty-seven different herbs, plants, and fruit peels on a cognac base. In the 1930s, the management decided to make a drier drink by blending Bénédictine with brandy. This after-dinner drink is B & B.

chartreuse

This famous liqueur is still made by the religious order that created it, Les Peres Chartreux, the Carthusian Fathers. The secret formula was devised in 1605 at the convent of the Grande Chartreuse at Grenoble, France. The formula was perfected in 1737 by a monk who was described as a "very clever apothecary." In 1903, the Carthusian Fathers were expelled from their monastery under a French law aimed at religious orders. They found refuge in another monastery of their order located in Tarragona, Spain, where they continued to produce their famous liqueur.

The French govenment tried, to no avail, to duplicate the formula. The company producing the imitation Chartreuse went nearly bankrupt, so some shrewd businessmen bought up all the shares and gained legal control of the company. They gave the stock to the fathers in Tarragona. Having recovered their distillery, the monks secretly returned to their country to make Chartruese. The French government chose to look the other way for some twenty years before officially repealing the expulsion decree.

There are two types of Chartreuse, yellow, around 86 proof, and green, 110 proof. Both are plant liqueurs made on a brandy base, spicy and aromatic in flavor, the green being the drier and more powerful of the two.

grand marnier

Grand Marnier, a brandy distilled along with macerated small green Curaçao oranges, is not found on all current after-dinner drink lists, but it is a longtime favorite and deserves mention.

sambuca

Occasionally, after a meal, with coffee, I am partial to Sambuca, preferably *nera,* black. It is an Italian licorice-tasting liqueur made from the elderbush, *sambucus* in Latin. Enjoy it *con mosca*—with a few coffee beans or "flies" floating on top.

tomorrow's POSTPRANDIALS

TEQUILA AND MESCAL

Not long ago, grappa was an alien rustic firewater; Scotch and bourbon were upscale cocktail favorites served with soda or branch water; and the postprandial list ran to liqueurs such as crème de menthe and Grand Marnier. What after-dinner drink fashion will tomorrow bring? It is fun to guess.

My bet would be on agave, a fleshy-leaved plant that is distilled to produce tequila and mescal. Tasting of herbs, vegetables, and fruit, tequila is immensely popular. Neither of these liquors is made from cactus, as is commonly thought. Called *maguey* in Spanish, agave is related to the aloe and lily family. There are hundreds of varieties of agave; some make a good spirit and some do not. True tequila is made entirely from the blue or *azul* agave which is cultivated specifically for this purpose.

Almost all true tequila comes from a region surrounding the town of Tequila, in the state of Jalisco.

But, alas, most of the tequila that goes into Margaritas and Sunrises is rotgut. Mexican law allows producers to slap a tequila label on any alcohol that has 51 percent distilled agave in it. The rest of it is rocket fuel made from sugarcane or worse. Most tequila drinkers have never tasted a premium 100 percent blue agave tequila.

And then there is mescal. The word comes from the pre-Hispanic Nahuatl language and means "agave." In the varied topography of the state of Oaxaca that encompasses mountains, plains, valleys, jungles, and the Pacific coast, many kinds of agave grow. Mescal is made from several varieties of this plant, including the sought-after blue, but unfortunately much of the liquor is cheap commercial stuff that has been chemically altered. The best is, well, like no other drink and can be hard to find.

Mescal is a more boisterous drink than tequila, and is made entirely by hand. The "fruit" of mescal can be the large blue agave or one of six other varieties of the plant. The local names are the giant *pulque maguey*, the *maguey tobala*, the sword-like *maguey espadin*, the horizontal *maguey tepestate*, the long *maguey larga*, and the rare wild species called *maguey silvestre*. All mescal comes from the state of Oaxaca. Mescal agave plants are propagated in small village garden plots for about two years and then are transplanted to mountain hillsides to grow on their own until harvest.

The making of these two native Mexican brandies is similar. The agave that goes into tequila does not mature until it reaches an age of eight to ten years. The agave's head, the *piña*, which resembles a giant pineapple and weighs in at well over one hundred pounds, is harvested from the plant and the stump is left. The heads contain a sweet sap called *aguamiel*, "honey water." The heads are split and steamed for a day at 200 degrees Fahrenheit. The *aguamiel* is then fermented, creating *madre pulque*, and distilled twice in copper pot stills. White tequilas are bottled immediately after distillation. The finer tequilas, the golds and the *anejos*, are aged in oak for one to three years, acquiring the qualities of wood and age just as cognac does.

The mescal *piñas* are treated somewhat differently. The whole heads are placed in a pit, covered with hot rocks and layers of agave leaves and palm fiber mats and earth. They bake for two or three days and then are crushed by a millstone turned by a burro or horse. This process gives mescal a taste that is distinct from tequila, even when the blue agave is used. The mash is fermented in wooden vats for up to a month. The mix of solids and liquid is distilled slowly in ceramic or copper stills. After the solids are removed, the *punta,* clear alcohol, is distilled once more. Then you have mescal.

The Tale of the Worm

Some mescals come with a worm in the bottle. This *gusano rojo,* red worm, lives in the agave. If left to its own devices it becomes a butterfly. The worm is popular in traditional Zapotec markets. It is eaten with tortillas or salt. In pre-Hispanic times, the worm was considered a condiment, an aphrodisiac, and even a source of strength and courage when eaten by a warrior.

One theory holds that it is added to mescal to assure the buyer of the lethal alcohol content of the liquor; another that it contributes to the flavor, smell, and color. One observer of the mescal scene says that to eat the worm will provide a jolt akin to the marijuana smoker's ingestion of the "roach."

The best mescals do not offer this snack.

If you're serious about tequila, drink only 100 percent blue agave, as indicated on the label. Also, make sure the tequila has a registration number that begins with the abbreviation NOM. This means the liquor has been bottled in Mexico, not in Texas or some other state where an importer might have a plant. One hundred percent blue agave is relatively rare; remember it takes about ten years to grow the plant before harvest. Some reliable brands are Chinaco, Jose Cuervo,

Patron, Porfidio, Sauza, and El Tesoro de Don Felipe. Expert F. Paul Pacult especially recommends Herradura, whose 225-year-old operation makes only 100 percent blue agave tequila from plants grown on his farm. It is aged in oak and estate bottled.

Some of the flavors Pacult finds in the best tequilas are chocolate, coffee, rose petal, citrus, anise, black pepper, asparagus, and fresh herbs. If I were tasting the best, I'd probably use the tulip-shaped wine glass tasters recommend for investigating the better expressions of the distiller's craft. But I confess a fondness for the thick, translucent Mexican glassware, shot and goblet types, that tequila and margaritas are served in.

Mescal comes in different ages and flavors. There is a Mescal Con Chili (with chili pepper) and a Crema de Mescal (infused with orange). The common kinds are mescal blanco, which has been bottled immediately after distillation. And, the notorious mescal *con gusano.* Some less common mescals are *anejo,* which has been aged in oak for at least six months, and up to four years. The connoisseur will be on the lookout for mescal *tobala,* which has been distilled in black ceramic containers and is often made from a rare wild variety of agave, and mescal *minero* (named after the silver miners who could afford this expensive liquor), which has been triple distilled. Minero is very expensive, and is considered by many to be the best mescal has to offer.

Some brand names you might look for are Beneva, Chagoya, and Fernando Romero Blas. Del Maguey Single Village Mezcal, an importer located in Taos, New Mexico, offers bottlings of several very upscale artisanal village mescals that go for about sixty dollars a bottle.

> ## Pulque's Progress
>
> An example of how far this staple ingredient of TexMex restaurant margarita machines has come toward the premium market is a tequila called Paradiso Añejo that has been produced in consultation with a master cognac blender and aged in French cognac barrels. It costs 100 dollars a bottle.

Afterword —À Votre Santé

The meal is ending. It has been a grand dinner, a celebration. It began with champagne, Veuve Cliquot, and proceeded through three courses. As an appetizer, ragout of asparagus and morels, accompanied by a crisp Chablis; a first course of ravioli of snails, washed down with an Alsatian Riesling; and a second, the classic *gigot*, leg of lamb with garlic sauce, accompanied by a full-bodied Cabernet from the Napa Valley. As if the meal so far didn't require enough gustatory decisions, its denouement will put you to the test. Cheese? Dessert? Both? What to drink with one or the other? Port? Dessert wine? And, afterward, cognac, grappa, or an eau de vie? A single malt Scotch? Cigars? The waiter approaches or the host turns to his guests. The before and during parts of the meal are over; now is the beginning of the end, the after.

The first choice is the cheese. Most gastronomes would not match cheese with an after-dinner drink, the one exception being Stilton with port. And maybe a few walnuts. The drink preferred with cheese is usually a full-bodied red wine.

that dessert wines would be served with dessert. But not so. Again, the experts, though in this case there are several exceptions, recommend a good sweet wine, whether dried, iced, or nobly rotten, be given a room of its own at the end of a meal. There are exceptions. The general rule is the wine should be as sweet or sweeter than the dessert or it will taste flat. Vin Santo is commonly served with *biscotti,* double-baked, nutty-flavored biscuits or cookies, which are dipped into the wine. Some other possibilities are Sauternes with mango (as observed before, Sauternes is often the beverage of choice with foie gras, a combination of sweet and fat that perhaps is the equivalent of double jeopardy in law). Ice cream could be paired with a lightly fortified Muscat wine, such as a Muscat de Beaumes-de-Venise. A fruit tart or pie might go well with a young citrusy Barsac or Sauternes. An intriguing non-competitive combination is bittersweet chocolate with a Maury sweet wine from Mas Amiel.

Despite the admonition that rules are made to be broken, the point is that after-dinner drinks are just that—after-dinner drinks, intended for enjoyment by their own, and on their own, after the plates have been cleared and the table crumbed, after dessert and coffee, with stimulating dining mates. What the coda is to music and the aurora borealis is to a perfect summer night in the north, a fine cognac, port, poire Williams, or Sauternes is to the end of a good meal in convivial company.

Cigars

The image of a great meal being topped off by brandy and cigars is a vivid one, and to many, tempting. But, alas, to the experts, and no offense to cigar buffs, a fine cognac and the best Havana has to offer are better enjoyed separately. A triple-digit investment in the bottle of booze and a double in the smoke will pay higher dividends if not treated as a mutual fund.

In-Dinner Drinks

Of course, almost all after-dinner drinks can be used in the preparation of food. Madeira makes a terrific sauce for meat, as does port; bourbon provides glazes and sparks bread pudding; cognac or brandy is the all purpose flambée; Calvados is imbibed by a heavenly cake called *cannelé de Bordeaux* made by Paris's Poujauran bakery; some swear by Scotch with smoked salmon; Quady's Black Muscat dessert wine figures in Paula Wolfert's recipe for Catalan estofat of beef; and it strikes me that if Grand Marnier can flavor a soufflé, so might any of the fruit eaux de vie. I don't recall ever seeing a recipe asking for a dollop of grappa or marc, not to mention Chartreuse or mescal, but I wouldn't be surprised if a few existed.

Selected Bibliography

Finigan, Robert. *Robert Finigan's Essentials of Wine.* New York: Alfred A. Knopf, 1987.

Grossman, Harold J. *Grossman's Guide to Wines, Beers, and Spirits.* Edited by Harriet Lembeck. New York: Macmillan, 1983.

Jeffers, H. Paul. *High Spirits.* New York: Lyons & Burford, 1997.

Kolpan, Steven, Brian H. Smith, Michael A Weiss. *Exploring Wine: The Culinary Institute of America's Complete Guide to Wines of the World.* New York: Van Nostrand Reinhold, 1996.

Lerner, Daniel. *Single Malt & Scotch Whisky.* New York: Black Dog & Leventhal, 1997.

Pacult, F. Paul. *Kindred Spirits: The Spirit Journal Guide to the World's Distilled Spirits and Fortified Wines.* New York: Hyperion, 1997.

Regan, Gary, and Mardee Haidin Regan. *The Book of Bourbon and Other Fine American Whiskeys.* Shelburne, Vermont: Chapters Publishing Ltd., 1995.

Robinson, Jancis, editor. *The Oxford Companion to Wine.* Oxford: Oxford University Press, 1997.

Root, Waverly. *The Food of France.* New York: Alfred A. Knopf, 1958.

Spence, Godfrey. *The Port Companion.* New York: Macmillan, 1997.

St. Pierre, Brian. *A Perfect Glass of Wine: Choosing, Serving, and Enjoying.* San Francisco: Chronicle Books, 1996.

AUTHOR'S NOTE

I recommend the following magazines for occasional articles on the subjects of this book: *Gourmet, Saveur, The Wine Spectator,* and *Bon Appétit.*

Use the Internet to seek out Web sites of producers, writers, and fans of individual beverages. Try any of the search engines by entering the name of the drink.

Index